BROADEN

YOUR

BECOMING

SURRENDERING THE FAMILIAR,
STEPPING INTO THE FULLNESS

BROADEN YOUR BECOMING

EMILY ORDONEZ

Book Cover by *the*BookDesigners
Illustrations used under license from Shutterstock.com

Published in Story City, Iowa

Paperback ISBN: 979-8-9896009-0-8
Hardcover ISBN: 979-8-9896009-1-5
EbookISBN: 979-8-9896009-2-2

Library of Congress Control Number: 2023923720

To the true author of my story, God,
who I simply write for —
and to the one reading this now,
who needs a touch of true life.

TABLE OF CONTENTS

INTRODUCTION

Ever since I was a little girl, I've loved gardens. I'd steal away to sit out in my small secluded sanctuary where I'd talk to God, process emotions, freely express my anger, or sing songs that resonated with my heart. The garden was a safe place, tucked away from the rest of the world. It also contained life. It was full of vibrant colors and beautiful sounds; it tapped into all my senses. Rays of light would shine through the leaves, and I could feel the gravel beneath my feet. I'd sit on a little bench made of wood, listen to the dove cooing and the water fountain spilling out, and smell the sweet fragrance of jasmine filling the air. It was no typical garden full of fruits, vegetables, and weeds as you'd assume. Instead, it was a small space cozily enveloped in lush greenery, fragrant flowers, and a buzz of beauty. It's what I imagined the Garden of Eden would feel like. A harmonious balance of life, growth, and belonging.

Fast forward to today. I still love gardens, but rarely do I get to bask in them. More often, I make my own spaces where I sit and soak and connect with my Creator. Maybe you love gardens and maybe you don't. You may resonate with the stillness, the enjoyment of the wild growth, and the essence of nature. Yet, maybe you don't. Maybe your sanctuary is indoors, looking at the sun from afar and lighting a candle because nature is just as allergic to you as you are to it. Whether your happy place is indoors or outdoors, active or passive, full of people or all alone, I'd like to suggest we all crave the same thing.

We crave the sort of belonging we get from enjoying and participating in the greatness around us. We crave to feel loose and free from commotion, and to rest in the beauty of reflection and connection. We desire to engage and embrace, having a balance of both in a world full of extremes. We desire fullness and to experience the utmost that is meant for us. We all have a yearning for *more;* a higher calling, a higher Being, a higher belonging. I'm here with good news. All three are accessible to you. All three are for you. A full and free life is not a myth, it is just often missed.

In the coming chapters, I want to introduce you to a different narrative — one that flips your ideas of identity, challenges the people and places of your surroundings, and frees you to a new reality that God has already given you. If you're skeptical, I welcome you. You're probably one of my favorite people. You've been gifted with an intelligent mind of pushback, but let me tell you. You have a Creator of intelligent design who was the most radical of His time. He gets you, He loves you, and He wants you. All will be revealed, you'll see. My hope is that this book releases you from backward religion and false realities and frees you to think differently and accurately.

INTRODUCTION

For those of you who know the Lord and have a personal relationship with Him, I welcome you. I love you too. But I will say, this book may challenge you as it did me. I'm preaching to the choir as I type these words on the page. Laws and legality are for the flesh; liberty and freedom are for the spirit. I believe God is in the process of freeing our spirits and loosening the strongholds that have kept our minds on our fallen humanity. How often do we talk about who we once were and not who we are now in Christ? We focus on the mess we have made rather than the masterpiece God is creating. Let this book help free your mind of captivity and loosen it to liken you to the heart and mind of Christ.

Finally, to my friends who are opposed to God. Those who feel like you have no right to pick up this book and wonder how or why God would ever love you. Or maybe you believe He doesn't even exist. I welcome you. I love you. I want you to read and enjoy it. The pages I write are not intended to convert you, but to draw you to the One who loves you and chose you. I hope that you see Jesus as one who is not limiting but instead liberating. As one who gives unconditionally instead of one who pries away relentlessly. Maybe you picked up this book and don't even know why; keep reading. Keep seeking. A single word can change a life. A single phrase, once implanted into your heart, can change the trajectory of your future. And I have a feeling God wants to do something super special in and through you by redefining what you've always known.

So, be challenged, be encouraged, be freed. Broaden the boundaries of who you are becoming by stretching your mind to what is already unfolding right before your eyes. Don't miss it; there's a calling and belonging and a Being that can't wait to see who you're becoming. I can't wait to journey alongside you. So, I invite you to step into the garden. I invite you to get into the space where your soul can find rest and your mind can find renewal. Linger in this place of beauty and balance that only comes from the Creator of all good things. By doing so, you will come to recognize the life that is not just present around you, but is most importantly within you.

CHAPTER 1

IDENTITY FROM INTIMACY

Cape Town, South Africa is one of the most vibrant and diverse places on earth. The hustle and bustle of the port city is full of market vendors, tourism, and the smell of fresh, salty air. The sights are pristine with the bright blue waves crashing into the foothills of rocky, rugged mountains. The coast is lined with many colorful houses and businesses that gather people within. The most interesting thing about this beautiful city is its culture. Since there are 11 different languages spoken and many religions and ethnic backgrounds, you can imagine the diverse beliefs and ways of life on display. It has led to a sort of "hippie culture" that's open to almost anything and everything. So many options to choose from, so many things to partner with. Who you decide to be and the way you choose to live that out is welcomed there. Beautifully chaotic, yes? Slightly unstable, maybe? Nevertheless, it is open and welcoming.

I was there with a group of friends in 2021, and we

absolutely loved it. We grew a heart for the culture and sensed a need for belonging that these people had. We met people from India, Europe, Australia, those who were on vacation, others who grew up there with hurts and ambitions, people who came for solitude, and others who chose to live homeless. Some believed in God, others in Zeus, and those who believed in nothing at all. It was almost as if it was a hub for people in search of belonging, and each person pursued it in the way they saw fit. I'm sure this kind of life can be seen wherever you go in the world, but it was very evident here on Muizenberg Beach, South Africa.

With this in mind, one day my friends and I decided to go show love to those we walked by on the boardwalk. We grabbed a white board and wrote "free spiritual readings." Now before you freak out on me, no, we were not practicing any form of voodoo or hand readings. We were actually there on mission for Jesus and decided to get creative with our form of evangelism. Let me explain — we wrote the message, walked with the white board visible to those we passed by, and waited for someone to ask. To our surprise, many people were excited and open to being "read." We told them we'd take one minute to be silent and see what we got about them to encourage their hearts. Little did they know, we were praying to God and asking Him what He wanted to say to that person. After the short silence, we'd communicate what we felt we received. Many times it was an aspect of their life, their personality, or their story that only God would know and He so kindly gave to us to share. For example, we approached a lady working at the train station, and after a moment of silence I felt the Lord nudge me to tell her she's an amazing mom and that God sees her. She wept and said she'd been praying that morning for God to send someone to encourage her since she has a teenage boy who's falling away from the faith. Oh, how good God is! And that was the pattern each time we went out to love people. Nine times out of ten, it hit home for them. Our response would absolutely blow their mind, bring tears to their eyes, and they'd ask the same question we'd gotten over and over again; "How'd you know that?" This would open up the door for us to share about Jesus and how there's a God that loves them and would take the time to speak directly into their life that day to make sure they were cared for.

You see, the heart cry of humanity is to be known and seen. We crave to be "read" by someone or something so that we can be affirmed that we're on the right path. We want to uncover something significant in ourselves, but many times need an outside source to truly unravel that mystery. I'm convinced that those who asked us for a "spiritual reading" are not the minority, they are actually the majority. They were just those who were bold enough to ask. However, the question is, who are we asking? Who are we going to in order that we might understand a little more of who we are, what we're made for, or if what we're doing is right? If ordinary people can be uplifted by those interceding on their behalf, how much more could we be encouraged if we went directly to the source: the Creator.

I am confident that whether you're reading this and feel ultra certain of your identity or you're reading this just wishing someone would understand you, there's a part of your soul that wants to know more. You question, "This can't be all there is to my life, right?" Right. You're asking the right questions, but where are you searching for your answers? I'm here to suggest that your true identity comes through direct intimacy with the One who formed you. God has placed a unique fingerprint on your form and developed a DNA unique to you alone. As you can imagine, fingerprints and DNA are complex things, complex concepts. You don't understand them in a day, and there's new revelations scientists are making about them each week. Continually uncovering, ever intriguing. Much like these are your identity. When I looked up the definition of "identity" it read, "The state of remaining the same one under varying conditions."[1] You may think this is contrary to the statement I said just before this; however, it is not. You see, who you are was already determined before you existed. You're just learning to now *be* the same one God spoke into being with an infinitely creative mind. Identity is *being* who you already *are*. So, if you're wondering if there's more to your character, more to your life, more to your dreams, more to your becoming, I'd reply with a resounding yes. But the answer, the more of which you seek, the person you hope to be, is found through intimacy with Jesus.

The word "intimacy" may make you squirm or think of something only intended for a romantic couple. However, this is not the type of intimacy I'm talking about. I'm speaking of the one that relates to closeness, nearness, friendship, familiarity. When you cozy up and get familiar with the God who formed you and knows you better than you know yourself, you're cozying up to the person you wish to become at the same time. A combination of things we achieve and receive develop our dignity and pride, but it is truly only God who defines us. He's read you ten thousand times over and has studied you — all of you. You like to study the parts of your life you enjoy and nitpick the parts you wish were better. However, what about the deep parts of your soul that haven't yet been uncovered? What if the more in you is only accessible through the supernatural work of the Holy Spirit of God? How do we tap into that deep well of knowledge and discovery? I believe it's through a mind of mystery that drives us toward intimacy and in consequence, discovery of our identity.

So how do we keep our hearts hungry for more? How do we grow closer to the Creator of the universe in the mundane of our days? Well, let me ask you a very simple question I like to ask my friends: What do you love to do? What makes your heart come alive? Where do you feel most at peace? Do that thing. Go get into your happy space, your so-called sanctuary, and call on God. He loves to meet you in these intimate, quiet places. When you're in a space where you feel unhindered, God reveals his Word that is equally non-cumbersome and life giving. Maybe you have to go on a run to clear your mind, and the Lord speaks truth right where you just made space in your head. Maybe you need to go to a coffee shop, get cozy in a corner, open up your journal and write your heart out until your hand cramps; only then are you able to receive what He has already written over your life. Or maybe you need to go with a friend and spill, vent, cry, or word vomit what's been circling in your brain the last week. Go for that hike, go take that long awaited nap, go bake your favorite treat, and invite God into it. The Lord loves to meet you in your favorite places and touch your heart there. Other times, He'll ask you to step outside your comfort zone and surrender your desires to uncover a layer of your heart that needs to be awakened. This could look like serving your neighbor, signing up for a connection group, or sitting still when all you want to do is move. Whichever boat you are in, here's the point. A lot of times we make connecting with Jesus super complicated, when He's made it so simple. We were created for the garden. Think of Adam and Eve. The first humans were formed and made for delightful and direct access to their Creator. All their senses were brought to life, everything was holy and pure, all things were for their enjoyment and under their care. They walked with God in the cool of the day and it was *perfect*. So what changes for us? Obviously, the world is no longer perfect, our bodies are not perfect, and our desires are tainted by sin. But through Jesus, we are given full access again to paradise, to get back to the garden of our hearts and minds, and connect with the One who saw us unstained, unhindered, fully delivered. By connecting with God in and through all things, even the hard things, we discover parts of Him and parts of ourselves we never would otherwise. Maybe you've been told you're fearfully and wonderfully made and you've memorized that verse over and over again, but do you believe it? Do you live like it's true? If you don't, what would it look like if you did? I know for myself, I've inhaled truth, sermons, words of affirmation, and even memorized scripture about identity, but it didn't become a reality until it hit me intimately. The mysteries of God also reveal mysteries of our being, and they're meant to be discovered.

Psalm 139:16-18 says,

> "You saw me before I was born. Every day of my life was recorded in your book. Every moment was laid out before a single day had passed. How precious are your thoughts about me, O God. They cannot be numbered! I can't even count them; they outnumber the grains of sand! And when I wake up, you are still with me!"[2]

THE MYSTERIES OF GOD ALSO REVEAL MYSTERIES OF OUR BEING, **AND THEY'RE MEANT TO BE DISCOVERED.**

Man, how beautiful is that verse? God has not only *read* you, but He *wrote* you. His thoughts about you are endless! They number more than the grains of sand! I don't know about you, but if that's true, I'd be asking God a lot more questions about myself and my purpose rather than assuming I have it all figured out. I'd connect with Him more in those quiet, pleasurable spaces, get on my knees, and seek out His infinite mind. I'd take a lot more opportunities and step into more unknowns, knowing that my God goes before me and has readied me for that moment, even if I feel unsteady myself. If God has spoken it over you and has called you into something, no one can take that away. If He has declared something about your identity, nobody can discourage you from that or stop you from stepping into your beautiful becoming. I challenge you to ask God this simple question, whether you feel close to Him right now or not: "Lord, what do you think of me?" Don't fill in what you think He should say or how someone's defined you before, but let Him speak for Himself. He is kind and has a still, small voice. Now, jot it down. Allow Him to speak into the crevices of your heart that you haven't let anyone touch, and reveal things about yourself you never thought were there. Maybe He brings to mind something He admires about you, maybe something He's already revealed and wants you to know again, something that's hard to swallow and needs refining, or maybe something entirely new that's blowing your mind. It's not selfish to seek God to know yourself. To know God and be known by Him is a beautiful thing that goes hand-in-hand. When you lose intimacy, you lose your identity. And when you lose identity, you weaken the intimacy you have with God and others. If you have a poor view of the Creator, you'll have a poor view of what He's created, yourself included. But if you have a glorious view of Him, you'll have a good and glorious view of who He crafted you to be and who he's created others to become as well. We are told to love others as we love ourselves; how are you doing with the latter part? Are you criticizing yourself and putting labels on your life before God even has a say? Then, you'll do the same to others. You'll limit others' growth when you feel stunted yourself; this is our stingy and stubborn flesh. But when you seek to know God and in turn know yourself, your mind will broaden and your whole being will be shaped. When you fully step into who you're created to be, you allow others to freely become all they are meant to be. So, let me ask you: is it more selfish to stay stunted and unaware, or awakened and empowered? I believe the latter is more loving. We cannot give to and encourage others what we have not yet uncovered ourselves. Let yourself go there with God and allow Him to blow your mind and change your life.

So let's talk for a moment about what hinders the view of who you are in your truest form. Is it comparison? Lies? Fear? Loss of friendship? A horrible act done to you? Some or all of these may be true. Let me tell you a story to really get to the root of all our hindrances. It was my freshman year at Roland-Story High School during a passing period. A tall upperclassmen girl came over to me, stopped me in my tracks, and exclaimed, "Oh my gosh, look at your legs! You have tiny little twig legs." Ouch, thanks girl. To be honest, I just chuckled and agreed, because what does a tiny little freshman do at that point? I didn't think much of it at the moment, but that one comment would change the trajectory of the way I thought of my body for the rest of my high school career, and sometimes still to this day. Okay, you may be thinking, that's a bit dramatic Emily, don't you think? No, not really. It wasn't necessarily the words she spoke, but it was the fact that I left a damaging seed unchecked in my heart for years on end. One comment from one day turned into a question in my mind that stuck with me for years: Is she right? Do I have tiny twig legs? And if that's the case, is that a bad thing? See, she didn't say whether I was beautiful or ugly, she never said the words "not enough," and she definitely never said to hit the gym. However, I allowed one silly comment to speak more than it was ever intended to speak. I allowed one little seed of insecurity to fester, build, grow, and eventually even turn into an idol. My friends, this is what happens when we don't go to our Maker for answers, but we turn to the world or ourselves. Many times we desire approval of people and perfection in the eyes of those we fear rather than accepting the truest form of us that was already loved, accepted, and established. When I sought out the wisdom of man to answer my questioning of identity, the answer came back as "do better, try harder, just do you." But when I sought the wisdom of God after years of believing lies, He tenderly spoke, "You were created in the image of God to worship Me, not to worship a created image of yourself." This broke me and is still undoing the tender and broken piece of my heart inside. But it is better to hurt from healing than hurt from the pain of insecurity.

IT IS BETTER TO HURT FROM HEALING
THAN HURT FROM THE PAIN OF INSECURITY.

A perfect example of this is from one of the greatest leaders in the Bible, Moses. God called Moses to lead the people of Israel out of slavery in Egypt. He was to go to the Pharaoh and plead with him to set God's people free. Moses, however, argued with the Lord because he was insecure of his speaking abilities. He gave God all the reasons why he shouldn't, yet God gave him the one reason he should: "I am who I am."[3] It was never about Moses' ability, it was about the Lord's calling and authority on his life. So Moses obeyed. Flash forward, Moses is met with another situation. Still leading the Israelites, God asks him to speak to a rock and make water spring forth since the people were thirsty in the wilderness. However, Moses decided to hit the rock, being the logical thing to do, and water came out of it. The people cheered, but God was not pleased. He said, "Because you did not trust in me enough to honor me as holy in the sight of the Israelites, you will not bring this community into the land I give them."[4] Ouch, that had to hurt. Moses was on the verge of leading the Israelites from slavery into the land of inheritance God promised them. However, since Moses didn't trust God enough in his weakness, he lost access. God said speak, and instead Moses struck. It doesn't say this specifically, but I believe Moses still had a root of insecurity when it came to public speaking. So what did he do? He turned to the miracles he was used to — using the staff God had given him to make change. And yet, God asked him to do something new. He asked to no longer rely on the staff, but to use his voice and create something miraculous. I believe God was wanting to grow and stretch Moses to believe in Him alone and in his God-given capability. However, Moses failed the test. He allowed this insecurity to limit his accessibility to his inheritance. The same could be true of you. You may be allowing a seed of insecurity from the past to limit you from the miracles, the authority, and the newness God has for you today.

Maybe you had a similar situation to my freshman nightmare or maybe you encountered something completely different. My friend, we cannot control what happens to us, but we can control how we respond. Are you allowing situations to become insecurities that then become idols? Or are you taking your weakness to the feet of Jesus and allowing Him to speak into your hurt? You see, insecurity and intimidation are thieves. My pain left me more intimidated by people than interested in God and what He spoke over me. Whether it's comparison, unforgiveness, hurt, intimidation, insecurity, or you fill in the blank. I need to tell you this: they are all thieves to distance you from those you're fearing and postponers of the person you ought to be becoming. Do not allow your heart to go unchecked even for a moment. I know, it is easier to wallow in your weakness than to wait on God's words over you. But trust me, friend, you are worth the truth. You are worth being poured into. That moment that was stolen from you is going to be restored back in full measure by the One who gave everything for you. You were bought with such a high price; honor God by giving Him all of you, even the parts you're ashamed of. You are perfectly unfinished and complex. Even as Jesus said it is finished and it is done, you are becoming undone in perfect love. You are fully forgiven, completely beloved. Your pages have already been written, you are just in the process of uncovering it. You are one-hundred percent unique and there are pieces of you still being discovered each day. Do not get trapped in comparing your process to another's. You will start comparing when you stop belonging. Sit down and just be. The answers you seek are in the questions you'll ask. Just make sure you're asking your Creator, rather than the deceiver.

Our enemy, Satan, is known as the father of lies. His one job is to distort truth and reality, to accuse you, to shame you, and to speak lies of destruction. Satan is sly and sickening, Jesus is kind and healing. Jesus gives you words of hope while Satan speaks words of deception. I plead with you; listen to the Father of Life rather than the father of lies. Both will try to cozy up to you, speak to you, and hold you as a father would. However, one father steals his way in while the other speaks and stirs patiently. One yells shame, while the other whispers peaceful yet assertive truth. One will hold you captive, the other will hold you upright. My hope is that you choose the latter. Oh how lovely is the Father of Life, the Father God, who knew you and knit you together before you tried to know yourself. His words are valid because they were the ones that inspired your very being. The enemy's words are void because they cannot create anything, only deprive the being that was already founded. The enemy will try to keep you in mind games, but God is not in those. God is fighting for your life, not playing with the life you've been given. Lies are loud, truth is sincere, and stillness is needed to discern which is which. So I'll reiterate it again: get into your quiet space. Clear your mind and give God room to speak to you. Your identity is at stake and if the enemy can warp your identity, he can warp your becoming and steal your rightful belonging in the sweet presence of Jesus. The first step is knowing God, but He wants to take you a step further to know yourself.

I will not ask you to live up to your calling; this makes it sound as if it were out of your reach. But I ask you to live into all that God has claimed over you. You have only dipped your toe into the vast array of what He has in store. Open the Word, still your soul, open your hands, ask away, and find identity and purpose in the Author of your story. He's been waiting to reveal it to you.

CHAPTER 2

PERMISSION > RESTRICTION

here's a movie that came out in 2021 called *Yes Day*.[1] It's a heartfelt comedy that shows the yearning of kids' hearts: freedom. They want to grow into their independence and wish their parents to say "yes" to all their hearts desires. Typically, the parents say "no" due to a fear of their children's heart motives. So the plot takes us through a family's journey of finding the balance between loving limitations and the kids' freedom to choose. Their compromise was a so-called "yes day." It was one day out of the year that the kids could come up with a list of things they wanted to do, and the parents' only response would have to be simply "yes." I find it funny what the kids put on their list: eat as much sugar as they possibly can, play in a paintball tournament, drive through a carwash with all the windows down, attend a concert, etc. All thrilling and enjoyable things, but without any limits to their experience. They wanted to feel something and they wanted to test the limits and expand the boundaries their parents had placed on their day-to-day life. The result is what we might expect. The kids ended up exhausted and sick and even hurt, yet they also learned to trust the heart of their parents. They realized that boundaries were for their good and that their mother and father didn't want to end their fun, but instead prolong it.

It may be funny to think about, but I believe our relationships with God are pretty similar. Whether you've trusted Him as your Savior or are skeptical of Him, we all at some point tend to think He's a limiting figure in our life. That God is there to keep us from life, when in reality He wishes to prolong it and fill it with good things. Our reality is that God has actually given us more permission than restriction. His heart from the beginning was for us to enjoy creation, to embrace and discover, to push limits, and press into the unknowns. He wanted us to taste and see how good He is, how good He made us, and how good the rest of creation is. Going back to the beginning of the Bible, we see the Garden of Eden. We recognize the first humans, Adam and Eve, and how they were created to walk with the Lord in the cool of the day. God gave them dominion, called them good, told them to multiply and subdue the earth, gave them trees to eat from and to look at, sun to bask in, and work to be fulfilled in. God gave them an abundance and only one limitation: do not eat of a single tree. The fruit from that tree would kill them, but the rest would fill them and bring them delight. I find it funny that like the kids from *Yes Day*, we naturally gravitate towards the boundary rather than the abundance of what is for us. Instead of trusting the goodness of God and trusting that He had given everything they needed, Adam and Eve chose the one tree He put a limit on. And with one act of distrust, the rest of us are tainted with sin and enticed by the same desires they were. We tend to view life through the lens of lack rather than the lens of love. I'm here to tell you that is not what was intended for us. The Lord created us to walk and rest and bask and expand boundaries and subdue. And yet, we find most people dragging, nagging, limiting, and being overcome.

OUR REALITY IS THAT GOD HAS ACTUALLY GIVEN US MORE PERMISSION THAN RESTRICTION.

When we follow after every single "yes" that our hearts beg and crave for, we think we're doing ourselves a favor. Yet, in actuality, our "yes" to our flesh is binding us to the human experience of indulgence that only leads us to deprivation. Like the children who wanted it all, and indeed received all that was on their list, we, too, end up hurt, exhausted, and burnt out. We realize we were never created to fill the places in our hearts that feel dead and bored, but we were made to seek the One who Created all things with the intent of enjoyment and fulfillment.

My friends, we may not be given an abundance of yeses, but we are given an abundance of access. The Lord is limitless, humanity is limited, and within a relationship with Him we are given full access to the truest pleasures of life — because we find that He is life itself. Adam and Eve didn't physically die in the garden when they chose to eat the forbidden fruit, but they spiritually died because they were separated from God through their disobedience. See, they went from still and fulfilled to searching and fearful. They lacked because they lost sight of the Lord, the Giver of their life. When we lose sight of the Giver and go after the gifts, we separate from sweet serenity. Maybe you've felt this in your own life. Maybe you've tried to indulge and ended up disheveled and deprived. You've gone after every single inclination of your heart, but found it's a dead end that only leads back to your broken self. But what if our fullness is found in a surrender to God's design? Psalm 16:5-8 says, "The boundary lines have fallen for me in pleasant places; surely I have a delightful inheritance. I will praise the Lord, who counsels me; even at night my heart instructs me. I keep my eyes always on the Lord. With him at my right hand, I will not be shaken."[2] I love this verse because the writer, David, delights in the Lord's given boundaries. He realized the Lord was not limiting, He was, rather, liberating. Let me paint you a picture.

One day in my quiet time with God, He showed me an imagery to match the heart of this verse. Imagine a gated pasture land that is expansive and beautiful. There's many sheep grazing and wandering. The shepherd is within this gated area with them, caring and keeping watch over them. However, there's one sheep that keeps gravitating towards the gate. It sees the vastness beyond and wants to jump the fence to prove its ability. It views life as an obstacle to overcome rather than a place to abide. What it doesn't know is that there are wolves, predators, and death waiting for it on the other side. Without the shepherd's oversight, it lacks protection, comfort, and wellbeing. The same is true of us. Are we much more complex than sheep? Yes. Do our abilities expand beyond any other creature on earth? Most definitely. Yet are we an exception to our need for defined direction? I don't believe so.

You see, God has given us the whole earth to explore, to expand upon, to uncover. We're given freedom to choose a career, choose friends, discover our hobbies, and develop our unique qualities. Our access to fullness is wherever our feet touch as we're walking with the One who shepherds and guides us. Our limit is that of never leaving His love and His Word, yet having all else open to our disposal. Love is limitless, and if God is love and He lives within, the limit to our living is broad. I've always lived my life saying, "Wild and free because of Christ in me." My heart is loose and limitless in the way I experience the goodness and beauty of this life I've been given. Walking in purity and walking in the Way does not restrict me, it actually enables me to become everything I was meant to be and more. Trusting in myself ends at my own capabilities, but trusting in the Greater Being, God, awakens me to His good plans and pleasure. I delight more in myself because I see a broader perspective. I see the untapped potential of others that wouldn't be possible without the subtle speaking of the Shepherd.

God doesn't just give us a "yes" day, He has given us a full "yes" in Christ Jesus. I like to think of the biggest "yes" day as the resurrection. When Jesus rose from the grave after being dead for three days, He showed His might and power that is unhindered. When we put our trust in Jesus, when we believe He is the real deal, we receive that same power. Nothing is impossible for God, and if that is true, then nothing is impossible for those who believe. Does this sound restricting to you? Jesus released all darkness and all shame and all limiting factors over your life through His death and resurrection. Now He's ushering you into a life beyond what you can think or even imagine. He wants to show you that His ways are even greater than your wishes. He doesn't just guide you selfishly, He has good plans for your life. You may have been told that God tells you to erase all your desires, to scratch your so-called "yes" day list. But I believe God put those deep desires in you in the first place, and that they're not necessarily contrary, they're just not comparable to His. You're not crazy for wanting to start that business, your dreams are not so big they cannot be reached, your desire for a spouse is not wrong, and that thought of being an influential figure in this world isn't insignificant. You're not wrong for wanting a big and fulfilling life. Yet heed the words of God, heed His direction, and keep in step with Him. He has drawn pleasant boundary lines for your life, He has an amazing inheritance He desires you to step into, and yet it cannot be in your own strength and own ways. He craves partnership. He's not demeaning and He's not passive; His direction is clear and kind, uplifting and giving. Do not totally neglect the inclinations in your heart, but instead surrender them to the ever-loving and all great God who can do even more with those desires than you ever could. He'll set you up with the right person, in the right place, at the right time. He'll use you in amazing and vast ways. Jesus will free you in your pursuit of full freedom. As you grow, as you become, don't rush the process and don't drag behind. Listen to the pitter patter inside you, the things that make you come alive, and ask God to not just tag along but to instruct, lead, and be what He's always meant to be: Lord.

JESUS WILL FREE YOU IN YOUR
PURSUIT OF FULL FREEDOM.

A lot of times we think this looks like our passivity and God's activity. However, I believe it's a give and take, an asking and answering, a directing and an obeying. We see this all throughout scripture and I hope you see it now through this example. Let's say you've just received a new fancy car and can't wait to take it out for a ride. Who would you put in the driver's seat? You or the most experienced driver you know? Would you hand your keys over in fear of wrecking but never enjoying the pleasure of driving? Or would you hop into the front seat with full gratitude and confidence, knowing you've learned enough to get going? It may be an odd analogy, but I think more of us take the first option in a spiritual sense. We'd rather have others, even good influential people, step into the driver's seat of our life, telling us how to live or what our lives should look like. And some of us would rather yell, "Jesus take the wheel," close our eyes, and hope everything turns out alright. But I believe God is raising up a generation that gets behind the wheel of their life, turns the key that Jesus has given them full access to, and drives. No, this is not to say you make all the turns and all the calls. Don't forget about the passenger seat. I believe God sits right next to you, whispering in your ear, "turn there," "stop here," and even "re-routing." He has entrusted us with our vehicle of life, and though He owns it, He delights to drive along right beside us, ever within us, always for us and our good. Without the Lord in the passenger seat, we'll miss the most scenic and adventurous routes there are. We'd miss the beauty because we're so focused on the fastest and easiest journey. I believe He's more about the growing and glorious view.

I think in our drive of life, we tend to fall into one of two ditches: we go into the side of either self-negligence or self-indulgence. To neglect, we try to push down our hopes and die to ourselves because we think that's what God wants. Those who do this focus so much on the dying, they neglect the becoming. Now, don't get me wrong. I know what the Bible says. We are called to crucify, aka die to, our flesh and sinful nature. However, ever since you put your trust in Jesus and allowed Him to make you new, He put a new heart inside of you. You've been renewed by His Holy Spirit and are now called a saint rather than a sinner. Yes, God has called you to put away who you once were; however, now He is more concerned with you becoming alive to who you are now. This uncovering of new is what I believe God wants more than a belittling of your past.

On the other hand, there's those who veer towards self-indulgence. They give into anything and everything, driving wherever they'd like, and end up lost, back at their starting point. They search after living and lose their belonging. So where's the middle ground you may ask? Listening and then doing. As God speaks and whispers into our ear direction and instruction, we willingly listen because we trust His heart. We've seen the amazing places He's led us to before, and we can't wait to listen and obey again. Yet somewhere along the way we get lazy and the thrill becomes more of a drill. We hit long stretches with no exits and it feels like He's forgotten about us. We so easily forget that we're truly not the ones with the map. He sees far beyond, we only see the next step. We must remember His goodness, recall every single pit stop where He filled us up, and the people we've met who were clearly divine interventions. Friend, you've been given unlimited permission to tap into the abundant life that is already set into motion. Stop waiting for others to give you an okay. Let me touch on this for a second.

Many times we look around us to obey the voice and calling within us. We check to make sure our path is making sense to those on the sidelines, but don't we want to be the ones on the field? We double-check that what we're pursuing is lining up with the influencers of our day. But if we want to be a world changer, why are we being a cultural succumber? What if it looks crazy? What if it doesn't make sense? What if those around me are shouting to slow down when I feel God saying full speed ahead? Go after it. Lock your eyes on the path set before you. You need not neglect your yearnings, yet don't chase them either. What you need is already within. Your brilliant story has already been written on the canvas of your heart. Seek the Lord and ask Him the way forward. Wisdom starts by fearing and honoring Him. Listen to His still small voice and make that turn, be okay with the pause, and move forward even if you only see one green light. He is delighting in the partnership of moving forward one "yes" at a time. And even in the things He says "no" to, there is always another "yes" on the other side. It's more fulfilling, more lovely, more life-giving than what you could picture. Trust Him in the mixture of your feelings. They are valid, but they aren't what make you victorious in the end. Allow the Holy Spirit to be your co-pilot, get behind the wheel, and drive. You've been given the permission to live a wildly wholesome life, and with the Lord it will be always full and right. Take David's advice; "I keep my eyes always on the Lord. With him at my right hand, I will not be shaken."[3] With Christ in the passenger seat, you will never be thrown off course. Instead, you will discover the path of permission intended for you all along.

CHAPTER 3

TENDENCIES, NOT REALITY

never did understand fasting. I wondered why you would purposely let yourself go hungry, limiting food and drink freely accessible for the taking. However, it was through practicing it that I began to fully understand it. Fasting feels unproductive in the moment, even counterintuitive. We want to enjoy all the good gifts God has given us and I'd usually give a hearty "Amen" to that. I believe we are meant to enjoy this life. Like I mentioned in the last chapter, we are given permission to. But I also believe we are first meant to enjoy the life that has been so graciously given and recieved within. You see, fasting is not God withholding His goodness from us. It is actually a choice we take to increase our awareness and intimacy with Him. When we limit our intake, we are awakened to the abundance that is already within.

When we're limited we realize we're weak. When we're weak we see we have a need, and our need drives us to our knees. On our knees we find sweet intimacy, and in intimacy we see its simplicity that we've replaced with our complexity. In simplicity, we find a sweet peace, a peace that makes us long for more. So, we search for the source of such peace, and in the process find our salvation and our sanctity: our true and abundant life in Jesus. I always love incorporating some sort of imagery, so think of it this way.

A sunflower always finds its source: the sun. Wherever the sun is, that is the way the sunflower is facing. It gravitates toward and reaches for the light because it knows without it, it can't survive. They grow tall and bright, thriving in community and producing fruitful seeds useful for many things. What would it be like to live in such a way? What if we were like sunflowers, stretching farther toward the light, eager to soak in all the substance one can from the only source that sustains: Christ. Or think of a vine. Jesus gave us this example in John 15, when He demonstrates our life as a branch and His life as the vine or the source. If a branch gets cut off from the main vine, it withers and dies, unable to produce any fruit. But if it remains connected and steadfast, it grows wildly and abundantly, yielding its fruit in its season. Jesus goes as far to say, "Apart from me, you can do nothing."[1]

You see, without a connection and intimate relationship with the Lord, we are merely another body walking this earth. We can walk and talk and make things happen, but there's no pep in the step, no life in the spirit, no real transformational movement. We can build things on earth, but they'll be shaken in the end if they're not built on the eternal. So what am I getting at? When we address our weaknesses instead of ignoring them, when we recognize our deep need for more intimacy instead of more intake, and we allow healthy limitations on our lives, we start thriving in the abundance of life available to us. When we realize that, yes, everything is permissible but not all things are beneficial[2], that is when real maturity has set in. We've already discussed the permissible portion – and what a great God we have who entrusts things to our stewardship. But now we're going to discuss the latter part: what is truly beneficial to our lives.

When I was in high school, I loved watching seasons of shows on Netflix. It was either *Friends*, *Virgin River*, or *Riverdale*. I would get hooked on the plot and feel immersed in the story myself, as if I was Rachel Green's bestie or Archie Andrew's girl. However, I realized this became a quick obsession of mine. I'd go to my room right after school or after a stressful day, plop down, and start an episode. One turned to three, and three turned into a whole season. It was "mindless" I told myself. Well, this is true. I was mindlessly intaking a whole plethora of ideas and signals and images that started creating an immature desire for sexual intimacy. One comment turned into a turn on, and next thing I knew I was acting out my desire in a way God never intended. I came home not planning to sin and hurt God's heart or hinder my young body, mind, and soul. I came home from school wanting an outlet, a source that would give a quick fix to all the emotions I felt inside. A big heart pang in high school was feeling lonely and overwhelmed, and somehow these shows put a Band-Aid where my heart cry resided. However, my seeking only led to sinning. Here's what I've found: what you desperately seek out is where your weakness can be found. We need to place our strongest fight on our weakest points and allow boundaries to be built for our benefit.

At some point in your life, you went from naturally seeking the source of your life, Jesus, to a counterfeit light of a screen, a job, a person, even a dream. It went from delight to desperation, and now you're in a hole you just don't know how to get out of. My friend, this is what happens when we don't believe we're best set up for abundance when there's healthy boundaries set in place. We call our temptations our tendencies because we've gotten so used to slipping down into the ruts we've made. The reality is, contrary to common belief, you have the power to change through the power of Christ in you.

I believe recognition is your first step. Recognize what you seek out that is not the Lord. Notice your patterns, your thoughts, and the tendencies you have when situations arise. What do you run to? Where does your mind go? What's your self-talk? What truths or lies bombard your brain? Note these things, but don't stop there. Recognition is the first step. We are not just about revelation, but about transformation. Invite God into the messiness, even if you feel like you've put a lower case god before Him. His heart may be broken but it is that very same love that will put your brokenness back together. Allow your heart to actually break for what breaks His. Then ask Him how to move forward. You see, I think a lot of times we don't want to ask because we don't want Him to actually be Lord of our life. We love the saving grace, but we despise the sanctifying work of the Spirit. It's messy, it's hard, and yes it takes our partnership and truthful walks. We may step forward to slide back again, but you're making progress. It was never about perfection, it was always about obedience. For me in my own personal life and struggle, this looked like stopping my episode splurges. I stopped watching my favorite shows because I knew they would trigger something within me, and God had gotten me to the point that temporary satisfaction was not worth my deadly sinning. I ended up deleting Netflix all together because I realized the app itself was a distraction and temptation. I had to learn to make every thought obedient to Christ.[3] If something caused me to stumble, I took Jesus's word for it and cut it off. Nothing is worth losing the sweet intimacy and pleasure of walking with the Lord. If you're not at that point, I implore you to start there. Is He worth it to you? Is true freedom worth it to you? Jesus thought you were worth it. He died so that you could see it. Now the question is, will you believe it?

One night I was really struggling and wrestling with the Lord. I wanted to sin so badly and give in, but I heard a still small voice say, "Emily, it is a choice. You have a choice in the matter." I prayed through the pangs of desperation and cravings I had created to my addiction. It felt painful to say no, to die to my flesh. But you know what happened? I slept that night, and when I awoke, from that morning on I never struggled with masturbation ever again. The Lord broke my chains in an act of total healing, but He needed my "yes" and my obedience to fully deliver me. What part of your life is God asking you to surrender into His hands? Are you willing to not just be forgiven, but totally delivered and set free? It is a costly price, but one with eternal treasures waiting for you on the other side. Heaven isn't just waiting for you after death, it has already come through Jesus and He wants you to taste the glory and freedom of it *tonight*. Will you allow Him?

You see, as humans, we let false humility or pride get in the way of our greatest need for God. We go from "woe is me" to "look at me," and yet notice they always end with *me*. But the heart posture that positions us to receive the life intended for us is meekness. To be meek is to be fully surrendered, to submit without resistance. In our healthiest state, we are meek unto God, receiving His full direction and guiding without any tension or withholding of our heart. When we surrender ourselves to His loving and mighty hand, all things start to make sense. What once was hard to break becomes easy to unravel. What once was hard to accomplish now seems possible, and you become able to do immeasurably more than you once imagined. What once was a burden now becomes a blessing because you see with a new lens of love. As a child, I always was labeled meek and saw it as a weakness. I believed timidity and meekness were the same thing, but this is not the case. If the Lord calls us to be meek and yet also declares we have a spirit not of timidity but of power, then they are not one in the same. Meekness is not a weakness, unless it is submitted under the wrong authority. Let me explain.

MEEKNESS IS NOT A WEAKNESS, UNLESS IT IS SUBMITTED UNDER THE WRONG AUTHORITY.

In the world's eyes, to be a meek person is to be a doormat, to back down, to comply with anything. But to be meek in the Lord's eyes is to surrender to His design and therefore forgo all others. It is not surrendering to people's opinions of you, it is not allowing people to walk all over you, and it's definitely not thinking of yourself as inferior. It is simply giving God your "yes" and believing all He says of you and stepping out into all He's called you to. When we have a meek heart posture, we are filled to the brim with the Holy Spirit's power, love, and self-discipline. When we're meek unto anything other than His leadership, we become powerless, filled with fear, and lose our sense of self control. When I accepted the label of meek as a weak thing, I surrendered to anything and everything. I believed I was weak, therefore the enemy had a foothold over me. And just to clarify, the enemy is not only Satan, but also the world and our own flesh. We battle against all three, yet you get to choose who you believe has authority. Under the enemy's reign, I was fearful of man, filled with envy, and gave into the sexual temptation of masturbation and lust. These were my so-called tendencies. However, when I began to see a meek spirit as a gift and not a cruelty, I stewarded such spirit under the tender and mighty hand of God. Under the Lord's reign, I'm filled with wisdom, clarity of mind, freedom, and an abundance of inheritance. This is my new reality. In Matthew chapter five, it says that the meek will inherit the earth.[4] God has a good and bountiful portion of life for you to uncover if only you would submit under His glorious design. His heart for you is to conquer and thrive, the enemy's scheme is for you to suffer and be enslaved. We are all meek unto something, followers before leaders. I pray God is your authority and guide.

Similar to being called meek, I always avoided feeling or being seen as weak. The sound of that word, *weak*, made me cringe. I tried to be the strong one for my family in hardship, strong spiritually for my peers, strong emotionally by showing no emotion, and strong physically because Lord knows I hated having so-called "twig legs." Weakness was the last thing I wanted to be known for and I still have a hard time accepting my faults. Any other perfectionists in the house? I believe setting high standards for ourselves is good and leaves room to grow, but expecting yourself to meet that bar every time is unrealistic and even damaging. Let me propose something I'd never realized until recently. What if weakness is just a state of being and not your identity? Identities are immovable, state of beings are fickle. So if weakness is a state that comes and goes, are we defined by our mistakes or are we defined by the truth? What if the realities of our being are not found in our tendencies but found rather in the tension of grace and obedience? I love how the apostle Paul approaches it in 2 Corinthians 12:1-10. He begs Jesus to take his weakness from him. I'm guessing he was a bit of a perfectionist like myself. But even more, I love how Jesus responds, "My grace is sufficient for you, for my power is made perfect in weakness." Paul responds with, "Therefore I will boast all the more gladly about my weaknesses, so that Christ's power may rest on me."[5] Our weakness does not deter God, and He is not offended by it so long as we take it to Him and surrender to His ever-loving and mighty hand. What we learn from this verse is that our weakness is a prerequisite to His grace and His power. If we didn't need God's intervention, wouldn't we be gods of ourselves? Weakness was never meant to separate us from our calling or our intimacy with God and others; it was actually intended to draw us closer. Now, does this mean we proudly claim our faulty defaults and say, "That's just who I am, take it or leave it!"? No, I think instead the Lord wants us to come to Him with our tendencies, our weaknesses, our stressors. In a surrendered, meek state, He is able to shape our faults into our victories. I'm able to boast about God's

OUR WEAKNESS IS A PREREQUISITE
TO HIS GRACE AND HIS POWER.

redeeming work in my life and the breaking of addiction because I realize, through His loving kindness, He turned my sin into my salvation. This is my new reality in Christ! I now have authority in the area of purity because I actually went to God in my weakness rather than continuing on in defiance. God's heart is for our fullness, not fake obedience. Stop pretending everything is fine as it is; stop allowing yourself to be claimed by the hurtful tendencies you assume; stop saying you are powerless when you have direct access to the all Powerful. Start claiming the identity God has already placed upon you: free, pure, lovely, chosen, able, delightful, holy. What would your life look like if you acted like that were true? How would you approach God differently if you knew He saw you not as the mess you made, but the masterpiece He created? If you're willing to do the hard, messy work of pruning, undoing, and rewiring your heart to your original design, I promise you will thrive. Even wildflowers that go unpruned become weeds. Don't allow your wild and free heart to go to that extreme. Surrender your desire for perfection and control, and that desire will be replaced with the One who is truly in control. Remember, your meekness is not a weakness, for true power comes from true surrender.

So far we've talked about weaknesses and harmful tendencies. But are all tendencies bad? No, I don't think so. I think God has given you beautiful tendencies that are part of your design. Sometimes we try to compete against and push down our God-given characteristics thinking they're wrong, but this only leads to false humility. This is opposite of the perfectionist pride we discussed earlier. You are allowed to truly enjoy your giftings. When you step into your God-given tendencies without avoiding or obsessing over them, you find a beautiful new becoming. For me, I naturally love public speaking, so I tend to gravitate toward the mic. I love using all my senses to experience life to the utmost, so you can find me touching anything and everything in a store, smelling candles, pointing out how beautiful something is, or wanting to try all the foods in all the places. Are these tendencies harmful? No, not at all. Can they become damaging if I don't set up boundaries? Of course. But don't let the enemy harp on you and say your natural inclinations are always wrong. Do you love to workout? Do it for God's glory. Do you love to eat and drink? Do it unto God's glory. Do you love time with people? Spend it gladly for His glory. To give Him glory is to simply honor Him in life through being you. In purity of heart and the enjoyment of life, we see glimpses of God in everything and demonstrate His glory by stepping into our calling. You cannot be truly recognizing and thanking God while foregoing Him at the same time. Develop self-control with the Holy Spirit's guide and continue reaching for His light. Step into what comes naturally, not abusing the grace of God but not neglecting it either. Find beauty in the balance, power in your weakness, enjoyment in your strength, and glory in your living. This, my friend, is your true reality.

CHAPTER 4

FULLNESS > FAMILIAR

just have to laugh coming into this chapter. As I sit here to write, I myself am still learning the lessons embedded in the text to follow. What I'm about to say is easier said than done, and it requires an immense amount of trust. It also requires a personal walk with Jesus. I'm talking about life; not just any ordinary life, but a wildly full and abundant one. It is not impossible but it is often replaced with complacency and familiarity. How many of us crave the feeling of fear? How many of us want to be pushed outside of our comfort zone? How many of us want to step into the unknown, trusting a Higher Power to be in control? Psh, nope. We all want to feel safe, secure, and settled. If we're honest, to settle is easier than to be movable. However, living things are growing things. They are not static, they are ever changing, ever moving, ever alive. If we want to flourish, we must be flexible. This is not easy, and I won't pretend it is. However, I have experienced it is worth it. And when I trust the Lord to live in abandon to His good plans for my life, it ends up immensely better than I could've dreamt. Let me give you a beautiful example that's close to my heart and is still unraveling in my life today.

In February of 2021, I took a flight to San Diego, California. This is where I grew up for seven years of my life and where many of my childhood friends still live. I was going to visit my very best friend and would fly back a week later. During that time, I was dating a very godly, respectable guy. It was fun and sweet, yet I lacked peace the entire relationship. I felt the Lord nudging my heart to break up with him but didn't know why. Why would I end something that seemed so good? I felt God say, "I have better for you." On my flight back to Iowa I contemplated this. I was overwhelmed and confused and couldn't seem to face the fact that this very same guy would pick me up from the airport later that day. As I wrestled with all of this in my mind, another man had boarded the same plane on his way back to Iowa. He had just been in Hawaii, working for some missionary friends. As he stepped toward his seat, he saw me sitting in the far back all by myself with a buttload of things tied to my waist and backpack. Yes, I overpacked. What's new? When he saw me, there was a nudge in his spirit to say hi. He'd proceed to arrange his luggage overhead ten times over just to get a better view and then walk back to the restroom to see if I'd catch his gaze. Well, after multiple attempts he had no luck. I was so immersed in my own world that I didn't see my fellow plane stalker. We flew back to Des Moines, got off the plane, and he watched me being greeted by my boyfriend at the time. Things didn't feel quite right in my heart, but he was familiar and I was okay with that at the time. The man from the plane was disappointed but moved along. Must've just been a fluke thing.

Well, a few months passed and within that timeframe I had broken up with my boyfriend. Everything within me and everyone around me screamed no, but my spirit pleaded yes. So, it was so. We broke things off just weeks before starting to work at the exact same summer camp. Yup, it was uncomfortable, and I felt very misunderstood. From the outside it looked like a dumb move, but I knew in my soul it was what God intended for me. Well, not too long after that emotional roller coaster, I started moving along with life, investing into my community, and looking forward to leaving for a missionary journey that fall. I was so excited and told God I was dedicated to learning what love looked like through His lens. I didn't want to start any relationship or dive into anything crazy significant before leaving for my 5 month missionary trip. Well, I like to think the Lord has a sense of humor, because He did the exact opposite. I definitely got to know His heart, but primarily through a special person.

One Sunday when I was not at church, a young man from Ecuador showed up to service. He was searching for a community and was late to the original church he was looking at, so decided to go to the nearest one, which was ours. Everyone was infatuated by his new presence and his eager heart to become involved. My dad was drawn to him and talked to him for a while, finding out that he, Leo, loved soccer, missions, and business. My amazing father put a plug in for me, letting him know I also love those same things and that he should join us at youth group that night. Being a youth leader, I showed up to the group to see this new "exotic" guy, as the youth girls called him. I walked towards him and was met by a sincere and sweet hello. Little did I know, I was the girl from the plane and he was my "stalker." Inside Leo's head, there were so many crazy connections happening and he heard the Lord say, "I'm giving you a second try, don't be shy." Crazy! It was one of those Hallmark movie moments that leaves you speechless. If you ever want to snag our story for one of your movies, we just ask for half the proceeds. I'm partially joking, but the moral of this whole story is that the Lord works wonders and truly writes the best stories. God knew I needed something super obvious to scream "He's the one!" And He knew Leo needed that first plane encounter to be bold in his pursuit toward me. Long story short, seven months later we were engaged, and seven months after that we were married. It's been a beautiful ride, and we expect nothing but love, joy, and adventure for years to come. Is it perfect? No. But far better than my own plan? Absolutely. Now when I share our story, I remind myself of God's faithfulness and the importance of our obedience. If I wouldn't have broken up with my boyfriend at the time, I wouldn't have been in the place to say "yes" to my now husband. If Leo wouldn't have reached out and gone to church to strengthen his faith, he wouldn't have encountered me. Our "yes" to God will sometimes require a "no" to someone or something else, but He has far better in store than what we could ask, think, or imagine. Our story is proof of Psalm 37:4, that when you "Delight yourself in the Lord, He will give you the desires of your heart."[1]

What is something God is asking you to lay down? What feels comfortable and familiar, but needs to be overcome by better and fuller? Do you believe you're in control of your life? That you have the keys to happiness and fulfillment? Or do you believe the One who created you also has the best intentions for you? Your answer to these questions will determine a lot: the direction of your life, the expanse of your growth, and the limits you'll go to trust His sovereign plan. You can stay comfortable within the boundaries of your mind, or you can go through the growing pains of stretching your imagination, your plans, your expectations and find something better on the other side. My husband, Leo, is not just a godly, honorable man, but he also shares the same vision, the same dreams for our future, and desires a similar lifestyle as me. He was the first man I truly wanted to serve and come alongside in life. The Lord blessed me with peace, even though our journey was messy and much harder to mesh. Two different cultures, two different languages, two different life backgrounds. But we have the same God, and with His blessing due to our obedience, it is wildly life-giving and enjoyable. God will never ask you to give up something without a plan to replace it with better and greater things. Does this disregard the tension of letting go of our mind map, our plans, our original hopes? No, all of that is very real. However, God does not disregard you completely, but instead partners with you in a powerful way with the perspective of what is truly best. We see a piece to the puzzle, a pattern in the artwork, but He sees the whole picture, the whole masterpiece. He will not let you walk by and miss it. God wants you to experience and embrace the fullness of the beautiful encounters, moments, and opportunities meant for you.

Does this mean God never wants us to feel comfortable or secure? Does it mean God doesn't enjoy our planning or pursuits? I don't think so. I think He enjoys seeing us put our best foot forward, yet to be flexible where that next step ends up being planted. A lot of times I think Jesus is standing on the waters of our lives, beckoning us to come, but we disregard Him as a ghost because it looks so unfamiliar to us. "No, that can't be God, it just doesn't make sense," we say. Whoa, did we just become our own god? Is our common sense the mark of our faith, or should our faith break the standards of all sense? Sometimes they align, and yet a lot of times they do not. Those are the moments we walk by faith and not by sight. Those are the times we ask the Lord for spiritual eyes. What looks impossible becomes possible within a trusting friendship with Jesus. Peter locked eyes with his teacher, his friend, his master. Faith led to action, and action deepened the friendship. Even in the sinking, Peter found his ever-present support was the same One beckoning him out onto the waters. Because of our friendship with Jesus, we risk the faith steps, and we find that they weren't in fact risky at all. Why? Because Life itself is on our side. Stepping out in faith doesn't *not* hinder or put our lives at risk, but instead it awakens the very Life inside of you, ever beside you, always for you. I've said this of the Lord, and I'll say it again and again until you believe it's true. And honestly, until I believe it to be true. Because life is so much more than staying within the boat of complacency and comfort. It is meant to be free and full.

When we think of being full, we think of feasting on an incredible meal and having to unbutton our pants because it was just that good. Well, God also talks about giving us a feast in a spiritual sense. He fills us up with the richness of His goodness and mercy, despite any presence of lies or enemies. And when we consume all of what He intends for us, the belts on our minds, our souls, and our lives enlarge. When we feast on the resources put right in front of us — the fruit of the Holy Spirit, the storehouses of Heaven, the forgiveness of sin and the power of resurrection within us — we become someone empowered, capable, and ready for all we feel stirred to do or believe. Feelings are not our feast, reality and truth are. The real you is not a limited one, but a freed one. The real you is not a cumbersome one, it is a delightful one. The real you is not an incapable one, but an able one.

Can I give you another example of why you should trust God with your story? I've been blessed with experiences that put the glory of God on display, and those encounters are the ones that have brought me the most joy. It's a strenuous journey getting to the point of surrender, but once I get there it's the best place for me to be. It's the best place for you to be as well. Here's another example.

FEELINGS ARE NOT OUR FEAST,
REALITY AND TRUTH ARE.

It was my freshman year of college and I was worshiping my heart out, praising Jesus at a church's ministry night. This was a weekly occurrence for me; however, this night was different. All of sudden, as I sang the lyrics, it felt as though everything blacked out. I could faintly hear the worship music in the background, but it felt like I was the only one in the room. All of a sudden, a vision occurred. I saw that I was standing on a sandy shore, staring at the blue waves crashing into the bay. I was surrounded by beautiful, colorful houses, sandwiched in between mountains, and yet I stood alone on the beach. Suddenly, I looked down and I was holding a fishing net with nothing in it. I looked to the left and a man was holding the other side of the net. The man told me to set it down and as I did, a wooden boat full of darker-skinned people approached the beach. I went into the water, grabbed the boat, and helped pull them fully onto shore. I suddenly snapped out of the vision and that was the end of it. I was back in a big auditorium full of college students singing to the songs played on stage. Honestly, that vision excited me like crazy. I knew God's heart was all over this, and that He had a wild plan for me.

I decided to do some research. I had been looking into doing a missions school called Youth With a Mission, but as I scanned different locations, I found one school called "Refuge." As I looked through the school's pictures, I realized they matched the vision God had given me. It was in Greece, some place I'd been dying to go to for years. The specific location was an island called Lesvos, and it showed wooden boats of dark-skinned people being pulled onto shore. On top of that, the island had colorful houses to match my vision! I got so stinking excited. I jumped to conclusions and exclaimed, "This is where I'm going! This is it!" It was so clear to me. I drove home that night and blurted to my parents right when I got home, "I'm going to Greece!" Now remember, this was my freshman year of college, and I was one semester away from getting my Associates degree. My parents were supportive, but advised me to wait until I finished out my degree. I complied and waited. During the waiting season, I continued to tell everyone I was going to Greece. I consistently messaged the YWAM base until they got sick of me, and followed up on their Instagram posts so much so that I was alerted when any news came up. You now know why I was devastated to find out the school I had plans to attend got canceled due to Covid. The whole year leading up to this big moment slipped away in seconds. *I missed my opportunity*, I thought. My heart was set on helping refugees in Lesvos, Greece. This is what God showed me, and now I look like a fool to the world. How could He do this to me? Or was it actually my missed opportunity?

A plethora of emotions washed over me. My dad had warned me not to exclaim my plans from the rooftop, so I was humiliated to re-do my support letter with pictures of Greece and a whole description of what my life would've been. I was honestly so fed up at that point and yearning to leave Iowa that I looked up the earliest YWAM school I could join. Looking into various locations, I found one in Orlando, Florida. I applied and got accepted within 24 hours and jumped on the opportunity.

A few months later I was at their base, thriving with new friends and enjoying the school. Two months of lecture passed quickly, which ushered in the second phase of the school that focuses on sending students to the nations. Don't worry, I'm getting to my point here soon. Stick with me, it's a beautiful one. We had three nations to choose from: Mexico, Tanzania, and South Africa. I was hoping Greece was on that list, but nope, nada. I prayed and felt tugged between the options, but South Africa it was. I had an incredible team and after months of growing our relationship with God, we were sent to Cape Town to live out what we had learned. The day we flew in, we arrived right before sunset. Our little house that we stayed in was a walk from the beach, so we all ran down to catch the stunning views. We looked like little tourists for sure. We kicked off our shoes, ran into the sand, and felt the cool breeze in our hair. We stood on Muizenberg beach, a little cove at the tip of Africa, surrounded by mountains and colorful houses behind us. The sunset was absolutely stunning, and I just paused in deep awe, staring out into the waves. Then I heard this sweet, still whisper, "Do you realize where you are right now?" Whoa, this couldn't be. Was this really the fulfillment of my vision? Where's the wooden boat? The fishing net?

A week or so later, I attended a sermon at a local church. The pastor spoke about the disciples not catching any fish, but Jesus telling them to drop their net one more time and they caught a ton of fish. He correlated that to our own efforts. Hoping to be fruitful in our own strength, it's only when we rely on the Lord and trust Him, listening and dropping our net one more time that we yield the blessing and the fruit we've been waiting for. God brought to mind my vision right away. I had listened to the man holding the other side of the net in my hands and dropped the net with nothing in it. It was then that I looked up and saw the boat full of people. The Lord showed me in that moment that those people in my vision were the ones I'd be serving and sharing Christ with in Africa. "Refuge" wasn't a place or a school, it was the person of Jesus, and He was using me to pull them into that safety. Wow, isn't

God's good plan greater than our own? Had I missed the opportunity for Greece earlier? Maybe. But God redeemed my story nonetheless and brought to fulfillment the vision I had lost hope in. My God is good and He offers fullness over what our mind familiarizes itself with. May He do the same for you.

As I mentioned earlier, sometimes it takes the scenic route for me to really understand what God is doing. I could've understood the mission earlier, forgone all the heartache and questioning, but I wouldn't have truly been amazed by the outcome if I hadn't wrestled through the journey. Let me give a very practical example of this. In the past year I've done lots of hikes, some in South Africa, North Carolina, and even good ole Iowa, but one of my favorites was in Fairbanks, Alaska. Leo and I started the trek in deep snow, and it truly only got worse from there. This mountain had a steep incline, the weather was negative 20 degrees, and the snow was up to our knees at this point. We finally had gotten to a little overlook and there were no other footprints past this point. It was a stunning view, overlooking the tops of trees and the deep ravines of other mountain ranges. Leo may have caused a mini avalanche in the process, but we won't talk about that. What I do want to share is the simple saying God whispered to me in that moment. He said, "Emily, the strenuous hike is worth the serene view." You see, the view was glorious, partly because of the visual beauty, but largely due to the stillness and peace we felt after the trek up the mountain. The fulfillment within me mixed with the elegance around me, making the entire trip worth it. My friend, you won't experience those life-giving, awe-inspiring moments without the daily climb of life. Sometimes it takes us huffing and puffing to get to a place of resting and enjoying. The paths God takes us on are not meant to make us weary, but to equip us, strengthen us, build character within us, and give us sweet peace on the other side. You may feel like you're on the uphill slope of things; the top seems unreachable, peace is far from you, and you feel knee deep in despair. Keep walking, keep listening. God goes before you, marking the path where your feeble knees are going to tread. The strenuous hike will not be in vain — there is a serene sight waiting for you. Where His footprints end is where your journey does, too. God is not misleading you, He is strengthening and guiding you. And yes, in our story, Leo did venture farther than the footsteps had wandered. As a result, the footing beneath us shook and caused us to run back onto the path. In the same way, when you venture off course and step farther than intended, God will shake you and awaken you back to safety. Plus, you'll have a good story to tell after the fact. But if you remember nothing else, remember to continue in steadfastness even when all seems hopeless or lost. The strenuous hike is worth the serene view, so keep moving, keep growing, keep living until you see it, too.

When talking about fullness, I can't help but think of the verse in John 10:10 that says, "The thief comes only to steal and kill and destroy; I have come that they may have life, and have it to the full."[2] Jesus spoke these sincere words when talking to spiritual leaders of His day, emphasizing He was the only true leader who brings abundant life through His sacrifice. It is through God's love that He brings us life. And it is through our love to Him that we get to experience the fullness of it. God says if we love Him, we will obey Him and His word.[3] An abundant life is not one of knowing all the right things, but it is walking and living it out in our day-to-day lives. If we truly believe something, it'll come out in our words and actions. If you desire a peaceful life but aren't willing to slow down and listen, then you truly don't believe peace is attainable. If you desire an addiction to be broken and pray day and night for it to leave, but you take no steps in the direction of healing, then you're wishing on something that you have no true belief in. Either we believe the Word of God in full or we don't. We either believe that through Jesus anything is possible, or we believe that simply nothing is. Don't get me wrong, there are seasons where our faith may waiver and we wonder what the Lord is doing or where we're going. However, the outcome and trajectory of our life is dependent on how much rent we give to God. Do we believe Him to fulfill every room of desire, need, and hope? Or do we block out spaces of our hearts because it's just too painful to be let down again? My friend, I want to speak to you with the same words God spoke to me: do not cap what you cannot control. Our desire for control is truly just a desire for the One who is ultimately in control. Do not block off the painful and almost unbelievable aspects of your life. Begin to loosen your grip and allow God in where you never thought it could be restored again.

DO NOT CAP
WHAT YOU CANNOT CONTROL.

Friend, you may just need the same encouragement I did. You are the apple of His eye. God sees you as His prized possession and He will never let you down. He is for you and not against you. He has abundant plans for your life if you're willing to find them in Him. Hide yourself in His refuge, in His strength, and most of all in His love. See yourself as He sees you: with generous eyes. He withholds nothing good from you and He's waiting for you to ask so that you may be filled to the brim. Be awakened to the abundant and available life within and tell your heart to beat again. Surrender the familiar and step into the fullness.

CHAPTER 5

FULLY AFFECTED = FULLY FREE

If you're like me, this title of "Fully affected equals fully Free" really intrigues you. It also may ruffle some of your feathers. You may be thinking I've taken this idea of fullness of life out of proportion. Allow me to explain. You may have been told your whole life not to be affected by things. We're often told to guard our hearts and minds, to push away negativity, to ignore our feelings because they're not fact, and to never be swayed by others' opinions. "Don't become affected by anything!" I feel this is what religion screams. And if you *are* affected, somehow that makes you a sinner and weak in your faith. However, I believe we haven't been taught to process and respond to situations properly, therefore we do so immaturely. I'm here to introduce a new way of thinking that I believe is exemplified through the perfect example, Jesus. I'm learning to believe that even in my wavering and in my limited perception of what's around me, I'm deepening roots within that can never be shaken.

When a baby tree is first beginning to grow, its trunk is surrounded by a support stake in order to guide it upright. The stake ensures no wind gust, pest, or heavy rain can shake the trunk or uproot its foundation. The baby tree is vulnerable and needs initial guidance. However, as it grows and deepens its roots, the stake is removed to fully expose the tree. It no longer has something to lean on, rather it must depend on its deepened roots to hold itself upright. It is not a cruel act to take away this artificial support. It is intended to benefit the young tree in the long run. It has to learn to sway in the wind, take in the rain, and stand firm against predators to prolong its life and continue growing. I'm guessing you know where I'm going with this analogy. Just as baby trees must learn to remain rooted amongst the elements, we must learn to remain grounded in our beliefs. We must draw from the depths of God's heart in order to stay steadfast and upright. There's a point where the things we once relied on get removed and we're required to solely rely on the roots we've grown deep down. We become exposed and therefore affected by what is happening around us and yet our strength and steadfastness are derived from deep within us, where Jesus is. If we truly search our hearts and minds and find nothing of substance to pull from, our foundation will be easily swayed by the winds of this world. You see, tree roots soak up the water and nutrients from the soil in which they're planted. They become strengthened from soaking in these things. Where and what are *your* roots saturated in? What do you run to when all else runs dry? Where do you find your comfort, strength, and peace? Do you muster up your own efforts? Do you try to lean on the strengths of others? Or do you seek and soak in the healthy and life-giving love of God over you? It is truly only His love that changes how we grow and live in our day-to-day lives.

In addition to the roots, are you allowing yourself to become affected by your surroundings? Are you allowing the storms to come and shake you up a bit? Are you learning the art of wrestling with your feelings, wrestling with the Lord, wrestling with the flesh, and coming out the other side stronger and more able to defend the truth you know so closely within? Or do you simply depend on the support stakes you've placed around your heart? Do you guard yourself so closely so that nothing comes in contact with your fragility? If this is the case my friend, I'm sad to say you're stunting your growth. To close yourself away from the rest of the world, to keep yourself fenced into your comfort zone, and to keep the so-called bumper rails up in your life, you're then keeping yourself from learning the hard lesson of steadfastness. I'm guessing you believe you do not have what it takes. To that, I would say you're probably right. You, in and of yourself, are not strong enough to withstand. However, the One in whom you're dependent and rooted in, is. He is able and willing to supply you with all you need to not just survive the storms, but to thrive through them. I admit that I sadly lived within the fences I'd built around my own heart for way too long.

I'm still in the process of tearing some down. I thought I was protecting myself by putting up walls towards others and hunkering down in the hard times. I labeled it as "guarding my heart." However, I was only stunting my growth. To truly guard yourself is to simply gird yourself with truth. It is not boxing yourself away and shutting off emotion. I'm not dismissing God's word that says to guard our hearts.[1] Quite the opposite. I'm simply debunking the

TO TRULY GUARD YOURSELF IS
TO SIMPLY GIRD YOURSELF WITH TRUTH.

false definition of what we've made it to be. Guarding your heart and mind is not naivety but proactive deepening of intimacy with God. It is within the embracing that you grow your ability to start trusting again. Trusting God, trusting others, and trusting yourself.

The definition of affected in its simplest form is being "deeply moved."[2] This is usually caused by an external force or happening. Is this wrong? I don't think so. It is not wrong to feel the pain of betrayal, to feel fear of the unknown, or to be awakened to the harsh realities of our broken world. In fact, our life experiences and interactions with others greatly shape the person we begin to become. This is not entirely bad. However, there's another definition that becomes harmful to our becoming. The word "impacted" is defined as being, "strongly or directly affected by something."[3] You see, to be touched or moved by something is different from being greatly impacted or redirected by that same thing. When Jesus walked this earth, He encountered many different events, people, circumstances, and places. Everywhere He went, He was affected by the environment He found Himself in. He could sense who was for Him and who was against Him. He could sense the spiritual atmosphere and could identify who in the room needed a touch of His presence. Jesus was deeply moved by people multiple times in the New Testament. People's pleas and faith moved His heart in such powerful ways. So to say Jesus was not affected or moved by surrounding factors would be naive. However, to say He was impacted and changed because of them would also be untrue. God's nature never changes, but His interactions with certain circumstances and people do. Why? Because He knew being fully affected would sometimes change the course of His direction. To sense where there was the greatest need meant to feel the depths of others' brokenness and meet them there. Jesus could've easily forgone the misery of humanity. Instead, He stepped into it expectantly. The greatest example of this kind of love that ushered in total freedom was the cross.

It was for the joy set before Him; the joy of redeeming our stories, of healing every broken part in you and me, in living with us, freeing us, and redefining our identities. It was this joy that brought Him to the point of death. And not just any death, a tortuous one full of mocking, shame, and utmost pain. Flogging, exposing, being betrayed. Jesus did not shy away from the pain of life and surrender — He actually succumbed to it. Jesus wept over Lazarus, Jesus sat in the dirt with a naked and ashamed woman, Jesus dripped beads of blood in immense stress in the garden before His crucifixion. And yet, He rose and came out victorious. He could've easily not felt anything and summoned angels to His aid at any moment. And yet, He didn't for our sake. He was the perfect example that being fully affected draws us into being fully free. The resurrection would've lost its power if Jesus wouldn't have endured till the end. The fullness of pain and death ushers in the fullness of resurrection power and life on the other side with Jesus. Pain might touch us, heartache may move us, and storms in life will wash up against us. However, none of these have the power to impact us in a greater measure than Jesus's love. The outcome of our growth and our lives is dependent on the depth of our dependence on Him. The greater we understand God's great love for us, the greater we can withstand what comes against us and embrace all that is meant for us. Ephesians 3:17-19 says it perfectly:

> "And I pray that Christ will be more and more at home in your hearts, living within you as you trust

in him. May your roots go down deep into the soil of God's marvelous love; and may you be able to feel and understand, as all God's children should, how long, how wide, how deep, and how high his love really is; and to experience this love for yourselves, though it is so great that you will never see the end of it or fully know or understand it. And so at last you will be filled up with God himself."[4]

I love this verse. As we experience God's love for ourselves, it becomes our grounding and even part of our very being. You may be thinking this truth is way simpler than the situation you find yourself in. You may think this is way easier said than done, and I would agree. To put down our guards, to deepen our roots, and to depend rather than defend isn't easy. Yet it's needed if you desire to mature past the point of simply protecting yourself. You see, if we desire to give ourselves to a greater cause, we must be willing to sway a bit to develop endurance and abundance. Fruit of our life will always follow our roots. If you crave a highly fruitful life, you must also deeply desire a firmly rooted one. We cannot expect one without the other. It's a beautiful thing, really. God will not push you or prod you into maturity, but He is willing to remove all your man-made boundaries if you're willing. He knows how much your heart is able to take on, how much you'll lose if you loosen your grip, and yet how much you'll gain when you go through the growing pains of trust.

In high school, I was a very guarded person. Halfway through my eighth-grade year, my parents decided we would move to good ole Iowa from beautiful San Diego, California. I'd grown up in Cali my whole life, and this transition would take me away from childhood friends, church family, and the best school I'd ever been a part of. Moving didn't make sense, yet it was where God was calling. So, my family obeyed and went through a whirlwind of emotions. Me, being the person I am, tried to be the fun and positive one. I told everyone to trust in the Lord, all the while my own faith was wavering. My friends, church, and school were the baby tree support stakes that needed to be removed for me to start growing roots in Christ and uncovering my unique identity. The journey of moving and reestablishing in a new place was the wind that deepened the strength of my faith. The woman I am today would not be the same without this transition. Did I seclude myself in the beginning? Yes, yes I did. I convinced myself that I needed no one and that nobody quite understood what I was going through. How could they? I didn't give people a chance and I sure as heck didn't give God a chance. But He slowly peeled back my layers. I found myself depressed and anxious, crying out to Him on the bathroom floor to feel something, to answer the question, "Why?" I found in that moment that dependence on God is not a weak thing, it is truly a necessity. I had leaned on the support stakes around my heart for way too long, and found my identity in the fence itself. When they fell, so did I. God had to get me to a point that my dependence and my source was not on my surroundings, but was within His very Being. He had to show me that being affected and being impacted, whether good or bad, were two very different things. If it crumbles you, it's started to become part of you. But if it touches or sways you only to reestablish you deeper in trueness and fullness, you've found your foundation to be rooted in the eternal.

I can't help but think of Jonah in the Bible. God called him to Nineveh, a frightening and great city, to confront them about their wickedness. Jonah, being a sensible yet scared man, ran and "hid" from God. He jumped onto a ship, hunkered below the deck, and fell asleep. However, God's righteous anger caused the sea to rage because of Jonah's disobedience. As frightened and persistent as Jonah was to run from his fear, the Lord was even more persistent to see His word fulfilled in and through Jonah's life. The conflicting storm that was occurring inside of Jonah now became a living, true storm that surrounded his ship of escape. God would not let him go on being ignorant and blind to His voice. Finally, being awakened by shipmates, Jonah confronted his reality and said to throw him overboard in order to appease God's anger. By doing so, Jonah was swallowed by the sea, only to be swallowed by a huge fish that God provided to save him. Okay, pause. Let's just acknowledge that this is a pretty wild story, and that our circumstances probably don't seem as morbid as this. However, don't we tend to do the same thing as Jonah? God speaks to us, lofty situations confront us, and we run. We'd rather be ignorant and comfortable than confrontational and adaptable. We hop onto a ship of escape that takes us so far, only to find a bigger storm that we've stirred up for ourselves. You see, isolation is easier than confrontation, but it's secluding and not freeing. Trying to push away from feelings of fear or pain is backing yourself into a corner instead of pressing through the barrier into breakthrough. It wasn't until Jonah jumped ship that he found true salvation and eventually freedom.

To finish the story, God didn't leave Jonah in the big fish forever. He only resided there long enough to face his resentment and declare his need for the Lord. As soon as the words "Salvation comes from the Lord"[5] came out of Jonah's mouth, God made the fish spit him out onto dry land. Soon afterward, the Lord commanded Jonah to go to Ninevah a second time, and he obeyed. See, Jonah started his journey with support stakes and fences placed around his heart and mind. He ran, hid, and hunkered down. This is an extreme we also fall victim to. Soon after, Jonah succumbed to the storm he was surrounded by and almost drowned. This option was also a form of quitting. However, it was only from the salvation of the Lord that Jonah truly surrendered. He allowed himself to be affected and inconvenienced so that those in Nineveh might be freed and forgiven. Sound familiar? Jesus also became affected by the weightiness of sin and shame so that we may live in freedom. Yet, He didn't stay in the grave. Neither did Jonah stay in the belly of a fish. God's intent is not for us to hide or to die. Instead, He desires us to thrive through a dependence on Him to confront the storm within. On the third day, Jesus rose. On the third day, Jonah was released. My friend, your day three of liberty is coming. God simply needs you to face your reality, say "yes" to Him, and begin the process of bending but not breaking. Surrender you support stakes and stay firm in the swaying. As my sister would say, "Blessed are the flexible, for they will not be broken."

So how do we practically live a girded rather than immaturely guarded life? Well, I like to think of the Holy Spirit as the membrane of our hearts. A cell membrane allows what goes in and out, a protective wall that enables passageway to that which is healthy and a barrier to that which is not. God in Spirit acts in the same way, protecting our hearts and minds, reminding us of the truth in which we were formed and created. Flexible and yet not permissible to everything. He will not allow us to wander or allow harm to come upon us unless we invite it in. It is God's doing to grow us and protect us and it's our job to listen and lean into Him. As we learn to stay in step with the Holy Spirit, we will grow spiritual fruit that reflects more of God's heart and mind. When storms and trials come and we feel shaken, we put on the full armor of God and choose to abide in His character rather than our fleshly nature. I think we either have two tendencies: we flee to the fences we've put up around our hearts, or we give into the storm itself and become destroyed either way. Maybe you relate to the analogy of wanting to protect yourself, but maybe you relate to the exact opposite. You may be too open and affected by everything and it has started to impact your very being. Staying in step with the Spirit will avoid either pitfall, that of avoiding or that of succumbing. Think of a wildflower, a tree, or a bird. Each one is affected by its surroundings, such as the weather or competitive neighbors. However, external factors don't change its *being*, it rather changes its *adaptability*. May we walk in the same way, with our eyes fixed on Jesus, "the author and perfecter of our faith."[6]

A practical way to live this out is going for literal walks with the Lord. God wants your honesty and transparency, not your forced complacency. Be real with Him. He already knows. The Holy Spirit whispered in my ear one day, "Hash it out with me." He's not afraid. I walked, I pleaded with Him to take away the pain, and I asked Him to change my circumstances. Did those things happen? Maybe over time. But honesty is not a free ticket to immediate change, it is a free ticket to immediate new perspective. God will give you new eyes to see as He sees and to set you up for the breakthrough that is beginning with your honesty. My friend, allow yourself to be affected by your circumstance and by your surroundings, but do not allow it to impact the very core root of your being. Be flexible but not always permissible. Listen and stay in step with the Spirit, trusting He will guard you as you gird yourself in His truth. We are both thermostats and thermometers. Evaluate the season you are in, but then allow

GOD WANTS YOUR HONESTY AND TRANSPARENCY, NOT YOUR FORCED COMPLACENCY.

change to begin from within and transform the circumstance you find yourself in. This way of living will free you from ignoring and will liberate you from succumbing. It will allow a freedom you never thought would be possible. Jesus is for you and not against you. He understands the pain and the stretching, and yet He will never let you encounter more than you can withstand with Him. Grow those roots deep in His love and watch that same love transform you. He will ask you to step back out again into the things that may have hurt you, to the people who might have misunderstood you, but only to redefine and redeem your heart within it. Through the good and bad, the delight and the hard, the windy and the still seasons, He is shaping you and teaching you to trust again. To trust Him, and to trust He will care for you as you reach out to others again. Deepen to broaden, and find freedom even through being affected.

CHAPTER 6

HEALTHY HUMANS

So far, we've touched on identity and intimacy within the context of us and God. We've discussed our personal life walks, weaknesses, and wants. But what about connections within a group setting? When and where does our unique individuality meet the complexity of the greater community? Out of all the wonders of life, what we crave the most is to feel accepted and connected… to belong. We cannot live within a bubble, me doing me and you doing you. When we are like this, we climb a cliff of self-achievement only to find a ledge that drops off at the top and ends in a crushed spirit. We were made to journey in unity of community, spurring one another on, aiding the weaker brother or sister, encouraging the stronger ones ahead of us, and finding contentment in the place and pace God's given you and me. Learning to walk out of your identity and be firmly founded in God is so important. However, learning to walk alongside your friend, your sister, your family, your "enemy," while still secure

and stable yourself, is one of the most freeing and important steps you'll take. You were never meant to journey this
life alone. If someone's told you you're better off as a lone
wolf, that is a lie that needs squashing through surrender.
Community is not easy; it's messy, and not always pretty,
but it is healing, growing, and most of all, needed.

A quote my husband always says is this, "If you want to
go fast, go alone. If you want to go far, go as a team."[1] I love
this. Endurance requires oneness with others. Longevity is
within the confines of a community. Burnout is when our
source is ourselves and we approach others as projects or
things to avoid rather than people to engage, befriend, and
help alongside the journey. Many of you have been hurt by
community, so you never want to put yourself out there
again. Trust me, I've been there. I've said the same state-
ments: "They'll never understand," "They don't get me,"
and "They're just not my type." My friend, you'll never
survive if you want your community to look exactly like
you. The complexity of community is what brings out your
originality even more. Broadening your palette to diversity
strengthens your individuality and accentuates your beauty.
A community isn't a comparison ground, an envious atmosphere, or a judgmental journey. Community is meant to be
celebrated, a ground for growing, and a journey of enjoying.
Living within it gives you a mission beyond your own reality. If our goal is to build our empires, climb our hills, get
to our own goals while dissembling others' along the way,
what have we created? An idol at best. My friend, to pursue

only your intentions to somehow prove yourself to God and others is putting yourself in the seat of God Himself; a seat we cannot bear the weight or glory of. On the flip side, when we partner with people and realize our mission

THE COMPLEXITY OF COMMUNITY IS WHAT BRINGS OUT YOUR ORIGINALITY EVEN MORE.

is beyond our own intentions, there's a level of purpose and freedom that we tap into. I'm not saying personal accomplishment is bad or necessarily wrong, but I am saying it should not be our only life goal. If we put down others to only pick ourselves up, we are missing the whole point. The golden rule still rings true in our lives today: treat others as you yourself wish to be treated. Even when we're not feeling it, even when we feel they don't deserve it, press in. If you're craving connection, if you hope for adventure, if you wish someone would just see and affirm you, then start connecting with the person next to you. Seek the small adventures of life and create one for someone you love. Start affirming the beauty you see in others and see yourself discover the greater beauty within yourself. My friend, create what you yourself crave. Life was always meant to be shared.

Have you ever heard about the Red Sea and the Dead Sea? The Red Sea is alive and active, full of living creatures and flowing into other bodies of water. There's a give and take, a natural commotion to this sea. On the other hand, the Dead Sea is exactly what it sounds like: dead. Nothing alive can flourish there, for there is no outlet. Rivers flow into this sea, but nothing is released, it simply sits and stores. Because of this, the water is toxic to life. It is simply a storage container of salty water rather than a vessel of life. How does this apply? Well, is your heart more like the Red Sea or the Dead Sea? Are you connected to the Lord, connected to community, receiving life and love with a clear outlet to also give it? Or are you simply a storage container, taking and taking and taking but never releasing? My friend, we as humans were designed to create more than we take in. If we sat around eating for 80 percent of our day but never moved, we'd feel bloated, weighed down, and purposeless. However, if we eat in spurts throughout our day and trust the meals to nourish our bodies for work, we live energetic, accomplished, and purposeful lives. In the same way, as we spend our quiet times and begin to see our identity and uncover our talents and giftings, we are also meant to use and steward such things. We were created to share those bright and beautiful aspects of ourselves. Your giftings are meant to be opened and once they are opened, they are also to be shared. I understand if you're a bit intimidated and I get that it's hard to put yourself out there. That's why it's so important who you give yourself to, who you open up to, and who you invest in. You were meant to shine for all to see, but you were only meant to give secret parts of yourself to a few. Be confident of your character but confide in your weakness with a trusted crew. Give compliments like they're candy but seek affirmation from those full of truth. Brighten people's day with the love of Christ but grow in love with someone who's equally yoked in Him.

You see, trust is at the core of a true community. It is something that you build, starting with you reaching out and laying a foundation. It requires effort to put ourselves out there, even if it means being denied a few times. My friend, Jesus was the perfect man and yet people hated Him. Take heart. Jesus was the greatest friend and lover of all time, and yet He only had 12 close friends, one of which betrayed Him. He knows your pain and sees your desire to be understood. But the rejection never kept Him from His connections, and neither should it keep you. If we fear others, we can never truly love them, for perfect love casts out fear.[2] Learn to love as the Lord does: unconditionally. And when people don't respond in the same way, it's okay. Bless them, forgive them, shake off the offense, and keep moving on. God will put the right people in your pathway. Being friendly to all doesn't mean you have to befriend them all. Be picky with your core people and be polite with those a little farther from you. Acceptance is the essence of friendship, yet influence is the outcome of it. Surrounding yourself with the right people is so important for this exact reason.

As you deepen your connection with those you choose to commune with on a daily basis, you start to pick up habits, attitudes, and character whether you like it or not. When you give your heart to friendships, they start to have a piece of you and tug you to become either your best or worst. Your closest chicas or buds should be those who fill your joy tank and fight for your fullness, and vice versa. Community should embody a culture of celebration, rather than one of comparison. Is this the kind of

ACCEPTANCE IS THE ESSENCE OF FRIENDSHIP,
YET INFLUENCE IS THE OUTCOME OF IT.

culture you're giving and consuming? Or do you need to grow in learning how to healthily champion your friends without being threatened yourself? Do you need to surround and gather people who both encourage you and yet are willing to offend your pride when the timing is right? You see, community is meant to be a healing space, not a harmful one. It is not a means to compete but rather to encourage and strengthen. We are all given pieces to the puzzle and when we lack to connect in a healthy way, we lose the bigger picture. The meaning of life is to love, and yet I feel I see more lust, longing, and nagging. We either seclude ourselves in fear of being hurt, or we seek out people to like us because we lack life and love inside of us. A healthy community is one of satisfied, yet broken, people coming together to benefit from each other's strengths, help one another in their weaknesses, and overcome the enemy by our love of one another. I am convinced that the world does not need more individuals to be confident of themselves for the sake of themselves. They need a community secure in the love they experience through the gift of friendship and connection with God and one another. As we unify, we beautify our essence and reach heights greater than we could've on our own. Jesus says it perfectly in John 13:34-35, "So now I am giving you a new commandment: Love each other. Just as I have loved you, you should love each other. Your love for one another will prove to the world that you are my disciples."[3] It is our love that proves to people all over that we are God's, and God is in us. Jesus cares more about your plans and purposes than you do. Trust that He holds your future and He created your individuality, but that it was not only intended to stay within your grasp and control. Your love and your resources will never be exhausted when you are tethered to His unending love and abundant storehouses. You lack no good thing, and neither does your brother or sister. And though you lack nothing, you need to be reminded of such things. Get connected into community and begin to see the fullness of Jesus who is for you and not against you. If God was a diamond, we all resemble a surface of such vibrancy and reflect a small fracture of His fullness. The world needs what you have, and you need what others have to offer. May love ground you, may community spur you on, and may God give you everything you need to live it all out.

A key component of community is the healing that comes through it. James 5:16 states, "Therefore, confess your sins to one another and pray for one another, that you may be healed. The prayer of a righteous person has great power as it is working."[4] I love this verse and have found it to be 100 percent true in my lifetime. We find absolute forgiveness through confessing our sin to Jesus and that act of surrender and repentance washes us clean. However, many times we still feel the guilt and shame because we walked the journey alone. But when we bring our sins and flaws into the light, suddenly we may be exposed, but we're no longer alone. There is a level of healing only accessible to us through community. That is crazy to me and honestly blows my mind! I believe it is in the kindness of Jesus that He intended us to become mended by confessing our mess to one another. Many times we want to do the opposite and hide away. This, my friend, is a tactic of the enemy and a response of the fallen flesh. But you are stronger than you think. It takes more humility and strength to reveal a weakness than it is to boast about your capabilities to loved ones. When I went through my struggle of both anxiety and masturbation, I automatically wanted to shut people and God out. I wanted people to see my goodness and not the brokenness I felt inside. However, it was only through my confession that I began to see breakthrough and was given accountability to tackle my shame and pride. Sin that stays in the dark festers and taunts, but when brought to the light, it gets consumed by God's great love displayed most clearly through those you trust. My friend, an awkward conversation is better than an addiction later down the road. Whether you think it's a big deal or not, bring it to a trusted and honorable friend or mentor. It will work wonders, I promise. And don't just take my word for it, take God's word for its worth. True relief and healing come through confessing your inner-most need with another.

THERE IS A LEVEL OF HEALING ONLY ACCESSIBLE TO US THROUGH COMMUNITY.

Healing also takes place in community as we seek the good of those around us. We are to feed off one another, spurring each other on. Another's strength should not hinder my weakness, and another's weakness should not puff up my strength. We are like batteries. When one is negative, the other is positive and they charge each other to create electricity. In the same way, even in our differences, community is meant to charge one another so that we can be effective lights in our life. Proverbs 14:30 says, "A tranquil heart gives life to the flesh, but envy makes the bones rot."[5] My friend, if we first do not find a safe place of healing within a healthy community, we cannot take a step further into intimacy and celebration. We give life to one another as we cultivate it through transparency and humility. Yet if we hold onto unforgiveness, insecurity, intimidation, or fear, it keeps us from true friendship and quickly turns into envy. We were never meant to look at another's strength and feel lessened by it. We were never meant to feel lack or alone in community, and yet so often we do. Why? Because we don't allow it to be what it was first intended for: a place for oneness, growth, openness, and healing. When we allow it to be just that, we can step further into a celebratory, uplifting atmosphere. You cannot truly admire that which you envy. We cannot fully give in love to one another if we're hating another's becoming just because we dread our own. Learn to love in light of being loved. Community is not a place to pick apart yourself, it is a place to become more of yourself. It was meant to usher in grace and growth, not competition and jealousy. The Word says that those things are devilish and not for God's people. So how do we walk a life of celebrating others rather than comparing ourselves to them? How do we share the mic with our brother or sister, knowing that our time in the light will come?

First of all, thank God for those around you. It seems so simple but thank Him for the ones you tend to feel insecure with. Learn to honor and admire them. Then ask God what is true about you. He never wants to leave you insecure and questioning your worth. His thoughts toward you are more than the sand pebbles on the seashore. His desire is not to leave you wondering about your identity but walking upon the shore certain of it. Ask God to search your heart and determine why you felt a ping of jealousy. Every bit of envy is attached to a deeper root of insecurity. Take time to pull that sucker out so that nothing can poison or keep you from a God-given community. Read Psalm 139 over yourself again and again until you believe it's true. Have Him search and know your heart until all that's left is truth and love.

Another place we may feel tension in community is within our judgment. We of course don't call it that, but at the core it's what it is. We tend to make up stories in our minds of why people do what they do. For example, we think someone is loud and bubbly because they're an attention seeker, or we think someone is insecure because they're quieter and an intrinsic thinker. We make up our minds about those around us and yet hope to God they don't do the same to us. This needs to stop. May we allow people permission to express themselves and learn their story before we make up our own. Let me give you an example in my own life.

I was working one morning at the Bible Camp I staff full time. It was a marriage retreat and I was singing the worship songs alongside this middle-aged couple. Well, let me tell ya, the husband had a set of lungs on him. He really belted those chords with total confidence and enthusiasm. Meanwhile, I was standing to the left quietly singing and soaking, starting to get slightly annoyed by his belting. These were my literal thoughts: "This guy wants attention for his decently good voice," "He's one of *those* worshipers," "Dude can you quiet down a bit please, I'm trying to soak over here." Okay, it may seem ridiculous but it's so true. Then suddenly I heard the still small voice of my Savior say, "Emily, do not let another's worship offend you." Woah. I was so focused on correcting another person's expression of worship to God that I wasn't even adorning Him myself. Looking back, I can see the reason I was so "offended" was because I myself lacked confidence in loudly praising God. I had been told all my life to share my voice but lacked the boldness to do so. Whatever insecurity we allow to grow in us will ultimately keep us from the special humans around us. I almost let that be the case. But after God spoke so kindly and sternly to me, I started to praise right alongside this guy and his wife. I felt a spirit of joy begin to well up within me. And then, I felt tugged to pray for them. Say what? I went from being annoyed and offended to joyful and sincerely concerned for them. I came to find out that they had been struggling to get pregnant, and praise seemed to be their only weapon. My friends, listen closely. The enemy will try to keep you offended by those you are meant to become connected with. Do not let his schemes prevail. Love without cause and allow God's point of view to change your own. As His Word says, "So from now on we regard no one from a worldly point of view."[6] Another version words it as our fleshly viewpoint. Our role is not to judge, to compare, or to belittle. These are stinkin' mind games that are meant to keep us occupied and on the sidelines of our faith. Get back on track, praise alongside your peers, and be open to what God wants to do. Allow people to share their own stories before you make up your own. Allow God to highlight and share His story for you before you get stuck in your own script for your life. In community, we find not only healing, but also encouragement and a reawakening of identity.

In contrast to the community we strive to create above, there's a very poor and unhealthy version of it that we've labeled as friendship. However, the friendships I'm about to describe are not true relationships at all. Our goal is to be a community of healthy humans, but instead we've settled to be a surface level, complacent, and provoking one. We cling to unhealthy people because they're the ones that make us feel some sort of belonging through their sarcastic and demeaning love. Have you ever heard someone say, "You know I love you when I make fun of you?" Yeah, me too. There's a healthy level of joking and definitely room for bantering. However, when those in your circle start to demean and lessen your character and worth because something within them is insecure, this is where boundaries are needed.

My friend, you are nobody's sidekick, you are not a ringleader, and you were never meant to be alone. A healthy community is one of equals sharing life together.

We are called to be kind to all, but not friends with all. It is not selfish to circle yourself with the right kind of people. You are able to extend grace while also extending your boundary towards someone. You see, kindness and niceness are not the same thing. This has taken me a long time to understand and I'm still learning this lesson. The fruit of the Spirit is kindness, which is to be graceful and good to another. Many times this does include being nice to someone, expressing sweetness and a smile. However, sometimes the kindest thing to do is speak the hard truth knowing it'll save their soul. Sometimes, the kindest thing is to give space and allow that sibling you've been hovering over room to find help themselves. Sometimes, the kindest thing to do is to say no. This is hard to learn, but it will protect your heart and sanity. If we do not draw healthy boundaries around lifeless things and people, that same poison will start to creep into us. Does that mean we don't associate with those we disagree with? Does that mean we don't befriend the hard of heart? Does that mean we don't respect those who are different from us? Absolutely not. However, respecting someone does not always mean succumbing to their pattern of life. Befriending someone doesn't necessarily mean being tied to that same someone. Associating doesn't have to equal agreeing. We love without limits, yet we grow deep within boundaries established within agreeability to God.

Sometimes, it's the other person we need to distance ourselves from so that we can become all we were made for. It also allows space to connect with others worthy and needing of our time. However, sometimes it's our own stubborn pride we need to distance ourselves from. For example, when Leo and I were first dating we took a little trip to his brother's graduation. On the flight back, I was wrestling with my thoughts and couldn't believe how different Leo and I could be, and how we experienced God in such different ways. I had concluded towards the end of the flight that I was right, he was wrong, and he'd just have to learn my ways; aka my way or the highway. In the stern yet sweet voice of Father God, He spoke to me clearly and said, "You really think you know how to love me best, don't you?" Okay, ouch. And yet, He was right. I had this idea of perfection and what relationships with God and one another should look like. However, each of us resembles an attribute of God and moves His heart in a specific and special way. Who am I to dictate what loving God and others best looks like? We are made to learn from one another and humble ourselves under God's broad understanding and love. Community was never meant to be a place of competition, coveting, or comparison, but rather one of growth, giving, and celebrating. Can we agree to strive for this kind of side-by-side lifestyle? Can we break the mold of society and broaden the definition of community? I truly believe when we start to see one another as brothers and sisters, worthy of the love we so deeply crave, many things will start to change. Love limitlessly, cultivate healthy boundaries, create what you crave, and celebrate others like it was your day job. Release yourself from any obligation and become the person God molded you to be with the people who already see and believe in you too. To be healthy humans, we need to exist within a healthy community. Whatever we reap we will sow, so pour into the people who you wish to grow and broaden with, and start today. It's never too late.

CHAPTER 7

PREFERENCE OR DEVOTION?

hat if I told you Jesus didn't want to go to the cross? Say WHAT? That's right, I thought it was crazy, too. But as I was meditating on scripture in the shower one day—you know how it is... shower thoughts—God revealed something so surreal to me. Let's take a look at the passage first.

> In Luke 22:39-42 it says, "And he came out and went, as was his custom, to the Mount of Olives, and the disciples followed him. And when he came to the place, he said to them, 'Pray that you may not enter into temptation.' And he withdrew from them about a stone's throw, and knelt down and prayed, saying, 'Father, if you are willing, remove this cup from me. Nevertheless, not my will, but yours, be done.'"[1]

Jesus in this passage was praying with His disciples, teaching them the way to resist temptation. What temptation would Jesus have been facing? To not endure the cross. He knew what was about to happen. He knew seconds later He would be arrested. In His own words, He asked God to take it away. Actually, that would've been His human will or preference. And yet, Jesus said, "Not my will, but yours, be done."[2] Jesus was devoted to Father God and His love for humanity rather than to His own wishes. Jesus was the ultimate act of love, showing He would give up everything, even His own sanity, blood, and life so that we could be saved and freed. The joy set before Jesus was not the cross itself, but it was the powerful redemption that would take place because of His devoted obedience.

My friend, if we want to broaden our becoming, if we want to become the fullest version of ourselves, we must learn to love as Jesus loved. His love was not one of mere preference, of surface level friendship, or even one of liking. Jesus's love stretches far beyond our imagination, to the point of dying for the very ones that would kill Him, to the very one who betrayed Him. Many times in our culture, we like to say, "Oh I love this" or "I'm so in love with him" or "I would die for an iced latte right now." But would we? Do we actually? You see, people say that the word "love" has been thrown around way too much and I'm just now beginning to understand why. Love is not merely a word, it is an action and a person. To love on a human scale is to like or prefer something or someone. As soon as a person steps on our toes, doesn't meet our expectations, or disregards our worth, we begin to lessen *their* worth and claim *them* as "unworthy" of our love.

I've noticed in my own life that the things and the relationships I "love" come very natural to me and are very enjoyable: coffee, walks with a bestie, and quality time. We develop a natural preference for what is pleasurable to us. Is this wrong or sinful? Nope, like I said, it's 100 percent natural. But at the same time, we must not cease to love what feels unnatural or even unenjoyable. Looking again at Jesus, I'm sure He had a ton of fun healing people of their limp legs or leprosy, and definitely a lot less fun casting out demons and carrying a cross. Both are acts of love, and yet the latter came more costly. The measure of our love and devotion is not marked by how much we find pleasure in giving it but is measured by the extent in which we are willing to give. If it was hard for Jesus, it will be hard for us, no doubt. To die to our flesh is no easy task, but the Spirit within you is willing. That's why He says to stay in step with the Spirit so we will not succumb to our sinful nature.

The first time I truly faced this inward struggle was as a camp counselor. I had a group of ten nine-year-olds, and we decided to go for a hike down a steep ravine and into the muddy creek. One of my girls lost her shoe and started hobbling down the rest of the hill into the water. She started complaining about the sharp rocks and how unenjoyable the trip was. Quite honestly, I struggled with empathy at that moment because I had told her to change shoes before we left. Flip flops weren't the brightest option for this kind of trek. However, I tried to give a simple, "I'm so sorry, keep going you'll be okay." This, however, was no aid to this little girl. On the inside, I felt the Spirit nudging me to help her, and yet I felt this inward voice saying, "But, what if I don't want to? Why would I give up my shoes for this dirty gross water when I told her in the first place to change?" Then, something beautiful happened. My co-counselor, though younger than me, decided to take off her good Chacos, give them to this young girl, and even carry the other shoe she had left. Wow, the pang of conviction and yet pride swelled up within me. In that moment, I saw clearly that love is an action, and grace is going above and beyond what is required of us. It is choosing to serve another without trying to preserve yourself. And guess what? My friend's feet were totally fine by the end of the trip. She might've felt a few sharp pokes from the rocks in the creek bed, but it didn't compare to the sharp pangs of regret in my heart. This is a small example of love but it left a big mark in my life. A few years pass by, and I'm met with a very similar situation. I attended a discipleship training school in October of 2021. I was worshiping alongside my now husband and his sister. Both of them grew up in a third world country, learning to be content and considerate. During the service, one of the leaders came up and invited us to lay down our shoes in the very front. It was a sign of surrender to God in order to get our heart posture in a place to worship freely. I was met with the same question: do I forgo my comfortability or do I succumb to it?

At first, I made up a million excuses in my mind. *Oh, my feet probably smell. Oh, this is honestly kinda awkward.* And yet, without missing a single beat, Leo and his sister were the first ones to take off and lay down their shoes. Again, wow. I realized, in that moment, that those who may not have a ton to give in the physical usually have a multitude of wealth in the spiritual. They understand that to love is to give, and that true fulfillment is not remaining in your comfort zone but instead coming alive in your surrendered devotion. My question for you is the same: Will you let yourself feel the tension of being worthy of love, and yet giving it without question? Will you choose to surrender your comfort and complacency to experience a life of vibrant love and generosity? I sure hope so.

You see, many times we believe we don't have enough to give. We believe the lie that loving God and even others is a chore. However, this is not the case at all. We were born from love to love. One time, a little girl I nannied was telling me about the horse Secretariat and how it had a heart five times bigger than the other horses. My first response? "Wow! That must have really weighed it down!" Her response? "No, actually that's what helped it win all its races!" That was a simple yet profound statement from a little girl. Secretariat's enlarged heart was not a burden, but it instead gave it the capacity of endurance to run its race well. What is our race in life? To love and be loved. And how do we do that well without getting burnt out? Allowing our hearts to expand in each and every circumstance in life. We like to not feel, we enjoy not being empathetic because that is a lot harder than shutting off emotions and only caring about your own circumstance. And yet, it is allowing ourselves to become part of a much bigger picture when the things weighing us down become the very things that allow us to run the race of love best. Our lack is another's strength, and our strength is another's lack. You were meant to surrender your strength so that someone may be able to experience love for the first time. When you feel as though your needs are not being met, go meet the needs of another and see how your tank fills up tenfold. By loving out of devotion rather than emotion, you are living the life Jesus intended for us to live. It is not always easy, but it will be fulfilling.

Here's what I've found. It is easier to like and prefer rather than lay aside and love. We scroll through Instagram everyday "liking" things and calling it love. We can even like and prefer people on apps while swiping away the rest. However, to truly love someone is to lay down your life, your preferences, your wants, and your expectations for them. Does this mean you become an invisible doormat that nobody sees or cares for? Absolutely not. But it does mean to live a radical life that loves without limit because your love comes from a limitless source. It is standing firmly upon your own identity while assuring others of theirs through the ways you care and prefer them. Love is an intentional pursuit, not a passive happening. You do not just fall into love, you grow into it. The best way to see that is within a marriage relationship. Even when Leo and I started dating, he was the first man I ever truly wanted to serve. This was honestly the telling factor that I had this small seed of love for him. In the beginning of our relationship, he would mop floors at a CrossFit gym in order to receive a membership there — such an innovative entrepreneur — I adore the man. Anywho, late one night, Leo had to go mop the floors at the gym because he had decided to stay and help with our church's youth group, pouring into kids and neglecting his own sleep. Right away, without skipping a beat and barely knowing the dude, I offered

LOVE IS AN INTENTIONAL PURSUIT,
NOT A PASSIVE HAPPENING.

to help him mop. I couldn't believe it myself. I had been so cautious with other guys times before, but seeing Leo lay down his night made me want to lay down mine. Love stirs up love; therefore, we do not need to worry when we'll next receive it. What you sow, you will reap. That was true for Leo, and yes, I began to crush on him hard. He taught me how to salsa as we "worked," dancing with mop heads to romantic music. Yeah, yeah, we're cheesy, I know. Anywho, all this is to say, love is a choice, and when you gladly choose it, you will consequently find it.

So, what about all the things we say we "love." For me, the list would be coffee, quality time, sunsets, rabbits, and farmers markets to name a few. Yours may be notes of affirmation, avocado toast, hiking, journaling, fishing, etc. Whatever it is you love, I want you to know they are not bad things. It's not even a sin to say you love them because honestly we've turned the word into a catchy phrase for strongly liking or preferring something. I'm right in the same boat as you, friend. God created us with amazing senses to enjoy things around us, to feel the warm fuzzies of a compliment, to savor delicious food, and to marvel at nature. We were created to experience pleasure, and yet pleasure and love are not two in the same. If this were the case, we would only consume and dive into an unhealthy cycle of sensuality. Love and pleasure are a beautiful pair but not a comparative one. Love trumps all things, and if we put our senses, our preferences, or our own pleasures before it, we miss the bigger picture. We were created not only to take in and enjoy life, but to live out the love of Jesus through the unique passions and giftings you possess. To love God and others with all we have involves creating that which we crave. It also involves giving what may not be 100 percent enjoyable, but definitely beneficial for another. For example, as I mentioned before, I love quality time and coffee. The two paired together are unbeatable in my opinion. However, my husband loves acts of service and stewardship. I could easily blow his preference off as boring, and he could easily nag me about my spending. However, we've learned to compromise by taking time to budget for coffee dates while productively planning for our future.

Let's take it a step deeper. I see a woman on the side of the street with her baby and she's asking for money to support her family. In this moment I could easily walk by with the excuse that I am not a giver and that it's just not my strong suit. Or, let's say we see a kid getting passively picked on, but we're not that great at confrontation and would rather slip by like the rest because it would be too awkward to stand up for him. How about a third scenario: your sister or close friend really needs to talk but you're at the busiest point of your day and "just can't." Do any of these sound familiar? I know they do to me. As embarrassing as it is to admit, I often pass by opportunities to love because they are too inconvenient and not what I'm naturally gifted at. But is this true love? I don't think so. Neither did Jesus. He said this: "There is no greater love than to lay down one's life for one's friends."[3] Are we willing to lay down our reputation, our preference, or our position to love another? To treat someone how we'd want to be treated?

You see, love can be oh-so-wonderful and pleasurable, and it also can be oh-so-painful and costly. Love is death and life, serving and enjoying, fasting and feasting, giving and withholding. This is why we love in action, rather than store and impart on our chosen occasion. Love does not always come wrapped in a pretty package, but it often comes in the moments where we're hard pressed and all we have left to give is what's left in the overflow of our hearts. My friend, what would spill out of your heart? I am not saying we will have this perfected in one day, but I am saying we can grow in the ways we say we love. We can watch Jesus' example, follow suit, and mold our heart to His as we walk in the way He did. Here's my challenge to help you with this. Each and every day, do one loving action you enjoy, and then go do one act of love you'd actually not prefer to do. For example, in my own life, I'd write an encouraging letter to someone, affirming them in truth because that is a way I find joy in loving another. On the same day, I'd choose to be joyfully interruptible. If someone stopped me amidst my duties, I'd stop, turn my feet towards them, make eye contact, and intently listen. This is not my tendency, but Jesus is teaching me that people are more important than projects. This kind of love is not easy but it is needed. Make a list for yourself of love actions that come easily and others that are harder to give. Then, go do them both. Little by little, you will learn to be flexible and to love in ways that are not just enjoyable to you, but also beneficial to the other person and the Kingdom of God. I'm rooting for you, Jesus believes in you, and someone is waiting for you. Go and be devoted to love.

Let's touch for a moment on what love's enemy is. Right away, if I asked you what the opposite of love is, you'd probably respond with hate. I, too, thought this, until I had a conversation with Leo one day. He brought up the verse in 1 John that says, "Perfect love casts out fear."[4] After meditating and thinking on this, we realized that the opposite of love really isn't hate; it is actually at the core *fear*. Let me draw this out for you. If you see someone at school or at the store and they look super intimidating to you, what's your initial response? For me, I try to ignore them and walk past as fast as I can. Instead of engaging, I avoid. Acting in my fear, I am not able to love people well because I've allowed passivity to guide me more than intentionality. If I fear I am not good enough, my eyes are on myself and I tend to mess up more than mas-

PERFECT LOVE WILL PUSH AWAY FEAR, AND YET FEAR WILL ALSO PUSH AWAY PERFECT LOVE.

ter anything, and there's a spiral built of even more fear and doubt. However, when love steps in, it illuminates our eyes and wraps us in the grandeur of goodness that goes beyond ourselves. In the simplest form, fear is selfish, and love is selfless. Perfect love will push away fear, and yet fear will also push away perfect love. It is our responsibility to choose which we will succumb to each day. Both fear and love entice a feeling within us, and yet both require an action that follows it. If you are running away more than you are pursuing, that is a good sign your fear has blinded you to the love God has for you and others. The whole verse in 1 John 4 reads, "There is no fear in love, but perfect love casts out fear. For fear has to do with punishment, and whoever fears has not been perfected in love."[5] If you think God is distant most of the time, waiting for the moments you've messed up and wanting to jump on you for it, I'd say fear has lied to you long enough. Love should never be forced out of fear. If you obey God out of duty, hoping He won't be mad at you, this is not perfect love but instead performed love. If you show love to other people because of a fear of what they may think of you, this is not perfect love either but pacified love. My friend, to love in full is to know and believe the fullness of love God has for you. To know you are seen, chosen, and beloved. If you're thinking right now, "Man I blew it," trust me; God's love can undo it. Jesus' love does not point fingers or condemn, it rather looks you in the eyes and says, "You have it in you, let's try again." Even if love looks messy at first, do it messy. Even if it's hard to receive love at first, try to, even through the awkwardness. You see, true and perfect love does not come all that naturally because we've been plagued with imperfect and scary love in the past. We've let our experience dictate and define what love should look like, and this counterfeit has become all too familiar. The truest form of love does not demand, but is patient. It does not seek revenge, but it reconciles peacefully. Love is not some sort of envious partnership, but is an empowering and selfless friendship. Get to know the attributes of love. For love is not just a thing or an action, but it is the person of Jesus. He is patient and kind and rejoices over you in truth. Do not let fear lie to you anymore, saying you are too messed up or too immature or too imperfect to receive and give love. God is not only devoted to you, but He truly prefers you. Allow His perfect love to consume you, knowing that it chose you before you chose it.

CHAPTER 8

THE DREAMER & DOER

Picture this: it's a warm sunny day in San Diego, California. My family and I are headed up to the mountains in our burgundy minivan, windows down and seats packed with tents, snacks, and fishing gear. As we pull into the wooded entrance of our campground, our little Peekapoo named Missy peeks her head out of the window. At the time, our pup was only a few years old, and yet thought she could take on the world. Missy loved the windows down, lapping her tongue in the breeze, so we honestly didn't think much of it. However, as we slowed down and approached check-in, something caught little Missy's eye. Before we could scream or pull her back in, she leaped out of the van's window, chasing after what appeared to be a full-sized turkey. Thankfully, the turkey sprinted in the other direction and we were able to retrieve our dog. As silly as it sounds, a lot of us are like our pup, Missy. We love to be the passenger, we enjoy watching out the window, embracing the cool breeze and sight-seeing along the journey. To trust the driver is a relaxing thing. However, a lot of times we get distracted by objects outside the car, and like Missy, we want to leap for things out of our reach. Here's the analogy I'm trying to create: your life is like a car, my friend. Many times, we want to ride shotgun because it's a much more passive and enjoyable view. However, you were created to clutch the wheel. As I've mentioned before, God owns it, you drive it, the Holy Spirit guides it; that is, your life, of course. In the same way, when we allow other people to drive our dreams, we become distracted by things around us, like new and moving strategies or people who are in our desired position. Consequently, we hop out on our journey right before we reach our destination because we've become distracted passengers rather than diligent drivers. My friend, I want you to know that your dreams are worth it and God implanted them specifically on your heart for a reason. You contain insight and a heart that no other person has for your specific desires. You were placed on this earth for such a time as this, and those deep dreams that have been bubbling up onto the surface do not go unseen. It's time to grip the wheel and go. So let's get into it.

So, you're a dreamer. You have visions, ideas, inspiration and yet still lack the how-to. You are highly excitable and yet very dependent on others. And then there's the doers.

You get things done, you have strategic plans to achieve, you catch the given vision and run with it. Yet still, you lack the heart and the why behind the what. Two extremes and yet one common vision: to bring beauty from ashes, light into darkness, good into bad. I'd like to call the two extremes the "abiders" and the "stewards." Trust me, I know this all too well. I am the one who sees the big picture. I love to be the visionary and the heartbeat behind the grinding. And yet, I usually hate the grind. You can call me the dream-filled abider. Then, there's my husband. He's the one that loves to get his hands dirty, put in the hours, and sacrifice the temporary for longevity because that is where true growth takes place. Please meet the steward. Yes, both seem so different and yet they make a complementary couple that could be unstoppable for the Kingdom of God. You see, we all have our tendencies and our preferences of how we operate and live out our dreams and duties. However, if our goal is still to broaden our becoming, we must learn to tap into both personas and experience the fullness that Christ died to give us. Just as faith without deeds is dead, your dream without action is also dead.[1] So what's the balance you might ask? Good question, I'm still learning it myself. But I will tell you a few lessons God has taught me along the way.

Jesus is described as a Vine in the New Testament and we are described as branches that feed off of said vine. Without it, or really Him, we cannot create fruit or do any good thing at all. So, when it comes to our plans, desires, and dreams, we must learn to abide in Jesus in order to receive a fresh and better vision. To gain Christ's heart for your dream is much better and bigger than what we could ever conjure up. He takes an even greater perspective, always working things for our good and yet ultimately His glory. To abide is to remain open handed, receiving

JUST AS FAITH WITHOUT DEEDS IS DEAD, YOUR DREAM WITHOUT ACTION IS ALSO DEAD

all the good things intended for us and releasing all the weeds, lies, and detours that are against us. It is staying in step with Jesus. On the flip side, to be a steward is to be a diligent servant of Christ. We are all entrusted with the gift of life, and His question to us is, what will we do with it? You were created for more than just to be saved. You were made to be saved, sanctified, and set free to go, do, and be all you were meant to do and to be. A steward is one who catches and clings onto the good gifts God has given them and then puts them to work. They multiply what has been sown into their souls. Now, let's look at the two together. Without abiding, there is no vision; without stewarding, there is no direction. Open your hands to whatever God has, and then learn to grip onto the gifts He places within them. You can receive all the clarity you want, but then comes the question, "So what?" Clarity does not bring about change, but rather gives you the realization to then react to. Let me give you a visual of this. Picture a grape vine that produces juicy fruit. You pluck a bunch of grapes and wash them in clean water. They are ripe and ready to be pressed into sweet wine. The thought of smooth, yummy wine is pleasurable and it's as if you can already taste it. Yet, you're burdened by the following thought: there's so much more work to do. The process of stomping, straining, and storing the wine is hard and cumbersome work. The question is, are you willing to do it? If we love the outcome and yet despise the process, we cut ourselves short and will never fully arrive. The same is true of your dreams. Both the abiding and the stewarding stage is important. Another little tidbit is that the finer the wine, the longer the storage time. It may feel like your process is taking forever. You may feel like you've done all you can do, and now you're just waiting for someone to give you the okay. Your dream feels like it's aging on the shelf. My friend, please remember. Your waiting can be intentional, and the fineness of the outcome will be worth it.

Let's say you're stuck. You have an idea but have no clue how to continue forward. Maybe you have absolutely no starting point and aren't naturally a dreamer. Both are okay. I feel as though we have an expectation of having all the answers ourselves. We have this idea that everything will click together perfectly like we've seen in the movies. My friend, the best place to start is to answer this one word: "Why?" The "why" behind everything you do, especially your dreams, will drive you forward with more zeal and passion than anything else. For those who claim Jesus as their Savior, may He also become your Lord, or leader. Our dreams and ambitions should always be targeted to seek and bring the Kingdom of God above all else. If perfection, profit, or success is our goal, we will be disappointed every time. However, if your goal first and foremost is to expand the Kingdom through your progress, you will always be filled. He will naturally bring about blessings when our "why" is set on Him. God is expansive, we are limited. Let Him broaden your ideas and dreams.

Many times, we can't think beyond our own capabilities, our own bank account, our own knowledge, our own credibility, and our own desires. However, God expands our minds to see beyond our own bubble. He sees a need in your community and wants to match your dream with that specific need. He sees the person that will partner with you and bring provision, as long as you would get out of your comfort zone and ask. He sees the exact location that has been empty for so long and is just waiting for a dreamer like you to inhabit it. Allow the Holy Spirit to highlight that which has been hidden to your finite mind. Allow the expanse to take place as you invite the Lord into the space of your heart and mind. Surrender control; He will always exceed your expectations and break your calculations. Trust me, this is not easy, and something I am continually learning. So, let's do it together. One decision, one step at a time. This is the first step.

SURRENDER CONTROL; **HE WILL ALWAYS EXCEED YOUR EXPECTATIONS** AND BREAK YOUR CALCULATIONS.

Next, use the windshield wiper technique. As a car has these nifty features to clear away rain, you have wipers of your own to wash away the fogginess of your mind. Every person's wipers look different, but that is what I want you to figure out for yourself. What clears your mind and empties it so that it may be filled with creative thoughts from the Creator? For me personally, my wipers are intentional worship, painting, running or reflective journaling. What is it for you? Once your mind is cleared and the fog has lifted, now you must move forward. This is when you use the headlight technique. Equip yourself with tools that give you a clear step forward. What will help you to make the next right step? Not ten or twenty steps ahead, but what will illuminate a clear path right in front of you? Again, for me, this is time in the Word of God, daily to-dos, and time blocking to focus on my dreams. Find out what helps you focus to shift you into action. It's okay if it takes some time, for it'll be worth it in the long run. Once you uncover your metaphorical windshield wipers and headlights, get to driving. Remember, God is calling you to grip the wheel and go with Him. Let's set ourselves up to do just that. As you go, record pivotal pit stops along your journey of life. Each one is marked by what it either gained for you or took from you, but each of them shaped you somehow. Pivotal points of your life have guided you thus far, and now you get to choose whether they will continue to guide you for the good or bad. In the past, you have pivoted due to external forces. Now you have learned that you have power within to pivot where the Lord is calling. You are the driver, and you get to choose where you stop to fuel up. With a clear mind and illuminated pathway, you are ready for the journey, my friend. You are empowered with the Spirit, and He will not allow you to get off course. May you allow Him to guide you into longevity and prosperity, building the Kingdom one step at a time.

To wrap it up, I want to leave you with this: you have a choice, my friend. The power within you is the power to choose. Jesus has entrusted His Spirit to you, and now you get to choose to walk with Him in authority or tug against Him in naivety. You can allow God to broaden your horizons and lead you into fruitful opportunities, or you can remain boxed into your limiting beliefs of inability and anxiety. You were given dreams too big for your capacity because you were always meant to depend on the One who is big enough to complete them. The very fact that you're unsure is the very same assurance that it is worth stepping into. It is said that the graveyard is the richest place in the world because many people died never stepping into their dreams and God-given possibilities. May you never stay stagnant in a tug between comparison and intimidation. These will never lead to life but will bury you before your lungs give out. Instead, be inspired and ignited. Choose to view others' success, not as a tease, but rather a test. Do not wish open opportunities away, but rather join in and learn from them. You can either lurk and stalk others' becoming, or you can choose to broaden and step into yours. You're no longer just a dreamer, but a doer. You know who you are, and you've taken the time needed to clear away distractions. You've received clarity and you have Divine permission. However, an uncovering of dignity must always meet a stepping stone into destiny. May your pivotal point be today.

CHAPTER 9

RELENTLESSLY GENEROUS

e started off talking about identity and how this ultimately is derived from intimacy with Creator God. In knowing more of Him, you come to know more of yourself. Whether you believe in Jesus or not, I hope you see my story and are inspired that maybe, just maybe, He is real and He is good. I hope you've begun to see that He is not a foreign figure up in the sky, but He is a personal Father and friend, who resides in your heart if you so let Him in. I hope you've noticed that, as He promises, God is for you and not against you. That more than the plans you can work up for your own life, the image you've crafted of yourself, or even the limits you thought could stop you in this world — there is a God that extends and broadens those boundaries to reveal to you a whole new reality. When you let Him in, you're no longer just a better version of you, you become a whole new you. It's as if you had your DNA swapped and it changed you from lowly to royal, embarrassed to unashamed, addicted to free, fearful to fearless. You've realized this to be true: "God has not given us a spirit of fear and timidity, but of power, love, and self-discipline."[1] Maybe for some of you, you've known these truths for a long time and need to truly rely on the grace that freed and saved you. Stop working for perfection when it has already been granted to you. Quit proving yourself when God has already marked you as approved. Allow His grace to strengthen you, as it should. No matter what journey you're on, or whichever chapter resonated most with you, I hope you ultimately experience the goodness and grace of Jesus in your life and allow Him to broaden who you continue to become. This is just the start, my friend.

You've believed that fate has determined your steps; however, God has shown you He is writing your story alongside you. He knows your next move, yet He allows you to choose it. With this newfound freedom it's easy to stay complacent, but please remain hungry for more. Isn't that why you picked up this book in the first place? If any of us feel as though we've arrived, we're only fooling ourselves. And yet, if you're constantly searching for new while discontent with the present, you're robbing yourself of joy. Remain consistent and always expectant. God is not the least bit finished with you, and He isn't in a rush to see the completed version of you either. If I can say one thing, it's that He loves the process and so should you. It's within the shaping and making of you that fullness of joy can be found. It's within the writing of your story that the mystery and awe of life is discovered. I once heard that shame will keep you in the past, fear holds you in the future, but gratitude keeps you grounded in the present. Recall the good in your story and keep seeking the Lord for more. Ask Him to weave the hurt into healing, the shame into victory, and your hopes into reality. Uncover the story He's already begun writing on your heart. The scariest place to be is stuck recalling, wondering, and wishing, rather than asking, seeking, and knocking. The latter is what you're created for. You may believe that your requests aren't important. You might be thinking you don't know how it could get better than this. Or maybe, you're wondering, "why try?" because He didn't answer in the past. Wherever you're at, I understand. I've been in all three scenarios and what I've found is that our experience of God may differ from time to time, but His heart and character never does. He never changes, and He wants to keep giving you goodness and life to the full-

THE SCARIEST PLACE TO BE IS STUCK RECALLING, WONDERING, AND WISHING, RATHER THAN ASKING, SEEKING, AND KNOCKING.

est. Hardship will come, experiences may block our perception of God, but He never runs out on us and never inflicts pain on His people. He is a God of promise, a God of love, and a God who gives good gifts. At the same time, He continues warning us, holding us, and helping us when we've received a harsh handling from the world. This does not mean He never disciplines us; however, it does mean even correction comes from a place of utmost good and love.

My encouragement to you is to keep dreaming and growing with the Lord. Lay out your requests before Him with thanksgiving and come before His throne with full confidence. Start writing down your bucket list again that you've left untouched since eighth grade. Why did the wonder and awe have to die? Being grown up doesn't mean giving up on childlike faith. Being grown in the faith is to become more and more childlike while becoming less and less childish. Allow your imagination to wander and allow God to receive it and deliver it through His awesome power. His plan was always to do life with you. He gave you grace to not only save you, but to grace you more for good works. What are those? What areas are you interested in but would never dare touch because you're too scared? Go there with God. I remember being afraid to write out a list for my dream guy because I didn't want to be too petty and I had been labeled as one with "too high of expectations." No joke, three months later, I was introduced to Leo and he literally met each of my specific requests to God. Not to mention, he was beautifully tan, which I told God would be just the cherry on top. He cares about the details and the little things. I also found it hard to believe God would ever answer my dream of going on a mission and visiting the beautiful place I had envisioned that one night at college worship. A year or so later, I found myself standing on the very banks my mind had dreamt, or more like God had dreamt up for me. It wasn't Greece, it was South Africa, and He fulfilled my heart cry with a hundred little miracles during that trip. Going back to freshman year of high school, I was terrified of public speaking and avoided the crowd. I would've never believed you if you were to tell me I'd be the top student in my collegiate speech class, and speaking on stages to peers and churches. Let me tell you friend, God can and He will exceed all your hopes and dreams. His thoughts are higher than your thoughts and His ways are higher than your ways.[2] He takes your hopes and brings them up to the next level. Upgrading can take a while, it can require you to clear storage in your heart and mind, and it needs you to be plugged into the right source. But once you receive the fullness and newness of what it has to offer - what Jesus has to offer - you will be running at greater capacities you never thought possible. I don't share my stories to boast about myself. Quite the opposite, actually. If you noticed in all three of my stories, I was doubtful, afraid, and unaware. However, I relied on the One bigger, stronger, and more powerful than me, who pulled my story together beautifully. He'll do the same for you if you allow Him.

One of my favorite songs is called "Make Room" by Community Music.[3] It speaks on removing things out of the way so that God can have a say. It calls us to release all of our familiar traditions and religions in order to reveal Jesus' way. If I could sum up the entirety of my heart for you, it would be the premise of that song. Better, greater, more, fuller; these are all the synonyms of your life now with God. Things do not become magically easier, but life will look a whole lot brighter. The question is, will you allow the time to recognize it and walk into it? If so, welcome to the club of the walking dead. Say what? That's right. We've died to our old way of life, our sinful nature, our limiting beliefs, our lied-to self, our no-good mentality. Now we're walking in the newness and fullness of the life

BETTER, GREATER, MORE, FULLER; THESE ARE ALL THE SYNONYMS OF YOUR LIFE NOW WITH GOD.

Jesus has given us. If you've never experienced this, today is the day. Ask Jesus for a new life: He'll extend it freely. Following Him will cost you in some way, whether that's comfort, convenience, or pride. But the cost will always be surpassed by His great reward of life. If you're in a different boat, where you've put your faith in Jesus but feel like the same old sinner from the first day you believed, I'm afraid not much has changed — you haven't realized the extent of newness God has given you. He turned you from a sinner to a saint, an orphan to an heir, a beggar to a brother. Now is not the time to mope, to remain stumped, to drag your feet in the mud and think less of yourself. Today is the day you come boldly to the throne of grace and ask God, "What is my assignment? Reveal it to me anew. Do what only you can do." This should be our daily heart posture. He will gift you a response, a friend, a kid to mentor, a man on the side of the road to love, a pesky coworker to be patient with, a country to travel to, a business to start, a relationship to mend. You name it, He'll speak it. Not only that, He'll show you the way forward one ask, one step, one move at a time. This is not a race to the finish, it is a race home. Home is where you rest, and home is beginning to happen within you. Heaven has dropped off its bags, kicked off its shoes, and moved in permanently. Our job? Stay in step with the Holy Spirit diligently. Focus on what He says "yes" to, trust Him when He says "no." Want to win the war for your mind and your life? Stop playing tug-of-war with the Lord and start submitting, making room, and getting on the move. God is relentless in His giving. We should be grateful in our receiving and thoughtful in our stewarding of such gifts. Ask Him what He's specifically graced you with and then allow His Spirit to help you steward it, multiply it, and bring life into places with it. "Freely you have received; freely give."[4]

I believe many times we block our ability to receive from God or hear from Him because we have a wrong view of Him. We go into our intentional times with Him saying, "Yeah, yeah. I know what you're going to say. I messed up again, I missed my quiet time, I... blah blah blah." It's all centered around "I" rather than His generous eye. Matthew 6:22-23 says, "The eye is the lamp of the body. So, if your eyes are healthy, your whole body will be full of light, but if your eyes are unhealthy, your whole body will be full of darkness. If then the light within you is darkness, how great is that darkness!"[5]

In Greek, the word healthy can be translated to generous. In the Bible, Jesus is referred to as the head, we are referred to as the body. His eye toward us is generous and not stingy. When you catch His gaze, when you believe you are the apple of His eye, truth will begin to illuminate within you and through you. When you begin to see Him as generous and gracious, you, in turn, will follow suit. If you desire a wild and free life, broadened beyond belief and full to the brim, begin to receive the good gifts God has implanted within you and provided around you. Ask Him for more opportunities to grow what you know, release what you hold, and step into what will stretch you. This may come through testing, trials, or victories. God will wink at you through the most evident, Spirit filled days, and He'll cry with you through the hardest, sanctifying ones, too. On the days that feel like just another Monday, He'll remind you to hold fast because a grand day and a good gift is coming. When you're feeling zero movement, fall into what you already know is true. Release the life you hold within, and allow your mind to grow beyond the boxes you've been limited to. A new life awaits you, grace will always come to meet you, and Jesus will continue to be generous toward you. Stay in step with Him, and He'll continue to overstep the laws of this life to replace it with a fullness of life from within.

CHAPTER 10

STEP INTO THE NEW YOU

We've come to the end, my friend. Except this most definitely is not your finish line, but just the beginning. You have a fresh start, a clean slate, and an open canvas. There are wide open fields in front of you with secrets to uncover, places to visit, dreams to unfold, and things to build. You've been given prompts and tools to step into a new chapter, the one you now get to write. I dedicate chapter 11 to you. Have at it. Write messy. Put down your dreams no matter how crazy or unreachable they may seem. Reach out to that friend. Go get in your quiet space and talk real with God. Allow the fullness of you to be revealed so that the fullness of Christ can take place within. Continue broadening who you are becoming — it's an ongoing growth cycle. It begins with humility, ends in power, and is connected by faith. Jesus is going to complete the good work He's started within you; I am very sure of that.[1] However, the ease of progression in your growth is dependent on your "yes" to Him. The ways in which God is growing and molding and shaping you isn't just for you, either. It's for those around you: your family, friends, nephews, mentees, kids, and co-workers. When they see your mind expanding, your habits changing, your heart growing, and your horizon broadening, they will want the same thing, too. When Jesus Christ fully gets ahold of you, He'll not just grasp your heart, but also the hearts of those around you. This is why it is no selfish thing to be intentional in who you're becoming. Ignorance is not bliss; it is belittling. You were made for empowering. The question simply is this: will you fear man, fear yourself, fear failure, *or* fear God? The first three will leave you scared, intimidated, insecure, and selfish. The last one, however, is a holy fear, peaceful and secure. You could honestly replace the word fear with "respect" or "honor." That which you honor is that which you regard in high esteem. If we elevate others, our own life, or fear itself to the highest standard, we are actually lowering ourselves to the bottom of the line. However, when we elevate and trust God's truth and love above all things, He picks us up and seats us on His lofty lap. We do not serve or fear Him to gain from Him, however. As I mentioned in the earlier chapter, He loves to give as we gaze in His eyes and live to honor Him. It is a beautiful give and take.

So let's talk about the ideal and new life God is offering you today. It breaks all boundaries, it's pure and life-giving, and it strengthens and equips you for everything He's placed on your heart to do. Sounds great, yes? Let's think of it as He is giving you a brand new set of shoes. They're pearly white, sleek and comfy, no stains, and they even smell good. You look at the shoes and admire them, you hold them in your hands, and you even thank God for them. However, in fear of getting them stained or dirty, you refuse to wear them. And when you do, you wear the shoes in no-threat areas that are mostly clean and com-

IGNORANCE IS NOT BLISS;
IT IS BELITTLING.
YOU WERE MADE FOR EMPOWERING.

fortable. Doesn't this sound like us? God has gifted us with a brand new life: clean, unstained, and beautiful. Yet, many times we don't even step into our new calling because we're scared of the messiness it will induce. We fear we'll screw it up, dull the shine, and wear the soles of our new self out. But isn't that what shoes are for? Isn't that what life is all about? God revealed to me that the wear and tear of your life shoes do not lessen their value, but instead reveal it. If you never walk in them, do you actually love them or do you just admire them? If you never live out the truth spoken over you or walk in the power God has given you, do you actually love your new life in Jesus, or do you simply admire it and choose to walk instead in your own ways? He has given you eternal shoes, not temporary ones. We weren't meant to cautiously wear them only on Sunday mornings and maybe Wednesday nights. We aren't meant to boast of how clean they are on the outside when a very scared person walks within them. We are meant to walk boldly in the new life given to us in all circumstances, whether clean or dirty, put together or messy, comfortable or very difficult. If we want to walk worthily, we must walk humbly.

In Ephesians 4:1-3, the Apostle Paul wrote, "I therefore, a prisoner for the Lord, urge you to walk in a manner worthy of the calling to which you have been called, with all humility and gentleness, with patience, bearing with one another in love, eager to maintain the unity of the Spirit in the bond of peace."[2]

We all have a similar calling — that of walking humbly and lovingly. However, we also have our own specific callings. One may be to teach, another to write, and yet another to build and create. Whatever it is, may it embellish your white shoes with color and vibrancy as you step into it messily and excitedly.

The ways God is beginning to move in your life will not look the same as they did in the past. He is broadening the boundaries, which means He will use tools, people, and experiences outside of them to grow you. You can expect discomfort, but you can also expect mighty new wonders. I love how C.S. Lewis put it in his book, *Prince Caspian*. The main character, Aslan, is a lion who represents Jesus, and he is speaking to a girl, Lucy, who represents you and me. Lucy is questioning why Aslan didn't come through, save, and answer her prayers in parallel to previous times in the past. He answers with this profound simplicity: "Things never happen the same way twice."[3] So true, and yet so often we expect real growth to come packaged with the exact same pretty bow as last time. Newness is not familiar, it is fashioned to create humility and dependency on the One who can ultimately bring about the transformation. Partner with where He has positioned you, step into where He is calling you, and never neglect the great process happening within you. Life is bubbling up, you're stepping into the reality of the new you, and wide-open possibilities are surrounding you. God is rooting for you, faith is coming alive in and through you, and you are becoming the fullest, liveliest, truest form of you. Broaden your becoming, and you will broaden the boundaries around you.

Abiding is the beginning of this new becoming. You must learn that none of this is a natural process that just occurs, but it's a deliberate choice to remain rooted and come into agreement with the person of Jesus. He chose you and spoke life into you, which then cleaned and readied you. However, now you get to choose Him by abiding and obeying Him above all else. This kind of trusted living will produce fruit in your life. Not fruit you eat with your mouth, but fruit that you see with your eyes and experience in your soul. Fruit of love, laughter, gracious endurance, steadfastness, self-control. God in His love chose you. His love was never meant for a select few, and yet only a few select it. I pray you are one of those. I pray you learn to abide in Him and His love every single day. Allow Him to teach you how to walk, how to talk, how to pray, how to obey. We don't know how this all was meant to look; the essence of perfection is only in One. Allow Jesus, the author and perfecter of your faith[4], to be the greatest teacher, mentor, and encourager in your life.

You are always being discipled and grown by something or someone; let it be the Lord. Where do you run? Where do you hide? Where do you draw from? Where do you abide? Questions like these reveal where your roots are planted and will help reveal where you need to uproot, replant, and grow deeper. Create open hands and start running into open spaces with the Lord. Then, get to creating with Him. Start crafting the life you were always intended to live through the wonder working power of Him who saved you from within. What God has promised over your life will never return void. He is faithful even when you feel faithless, and He is singing over you even when you feel you can't catch your breath. You are human, yes. You sin, yes. You may even feel incapable of this new life, yes. But you are now the home of Heaven and a friend of Jesus. You reign with the ring of His love and favor. He has claimed you and purchased you, not to be a controlled slave but to be a perfect and pure bride. You may feel the exact opposite of who Jesus says you are, but that is honestly the point. The disciples didn't feel ready. Peter felt very ordinary. Mary didn't feel lovely. Thomas could barely believe. And yet, Jesus continually called them higher into positions and places that stretched them, grew them, and one might even say broadened their becoming. If He calls the humble and the flexible, He is calling you. If He stirs the faint hearted into action, He is stirring you now. If He disciplines His children, He is lovingly convicting you now. If He humbles the proud, He is humbling you. And if He lifts the lowly, He is reassuring you of your identity. We ebb and flow, go through seasons and testings, have our tendencies, and have been labeled by classmates and family. However, God is in the work of creating

HE HAS SET YOU APART TO SET A NEW STRIDE FOR THE KINGDOM OF LIGHT.

a steady, new, beautiful person that He has already formed in you. You are breaking out of the boundaries you've set for yourself and growing into the fullness of the person He formed, spoke over, and delighted in since the beginning of time. He has set you apart to set a new stride for the Kingdom of light. You are making new pathways, new memories, new everything. You will receive pushback; you will go through *hard*. Nobody said growing pains were fun or that stretching was easy. However, everyone loves the end product of both. You are not just striving for an end product, but you are wrestling and winning the match of your lifetime. You are pinning the old you to the mat and rising victorious to the new person the Lord has crafted you to be. Do not boast in your broadening or even who you are becoming but boast in the One who developed and created you from the beginning. Go and tell your testimony. He will always be smiling as you continually give Him glory. In return, He will give you confidence from humility and fruitfulness from abiding. Jesus is not opposed to you and isn't ashamed of you. He is proud of you and wants to work with you, not just poke at you. He is gentle and lowly, even while being worthy of glory. Walk with Him daily. As you rub shoulders with Jesus, Jesus will start to rub off on you. Pass it on. Step into the good gifts and inheritance He's given you. Don't be afraid to ask for more and believe He has created a masterpiece in you that's capable of changing our world. Take time to broaden who you're becoming with God. In time, you will see fingerprints of what He's done in and through you and your partnership with Him in all the places you've been. Life will not just be multiplied in you, but also all around you. So start writing your story and step into the person you've already started becoming. Fullness is waiting, life is waiting, the new you is waiting, and a watching world needs what you have and who you are.

CHAPTER 11

(this one's for you, friend)

BROADEN YOUR BECOMING

BROADEN YOUR BECOMING

BROADEN YOUR BECOMING

ACKNOWLEDGMENTS

I first and foremost want to honor and give a million thanks to God. He gave me a new life, inspiration, ability, and the stories to craft a manuscript that speaks of His goodness and the fullness we receive through Jesus.

A huge thank you to my incredible husband, Leo, who relentlessly encouraged me every step of the journey. I don't think I would've had the grit or guts to write this book if it weren't for his daily love and support. I love you.

I am extremely grateful to Erin Weidemenn, who mentored me throughout the writing journey. Without the framework provided through her "Legacy Story Writing Academy," this book wouldn't be possible.

Many thanks to my sweet family who continually poured their love, time, and affirmation into the creation of this book. Their prayers were the fuel to my progress.

I would like to thank my "Spirit Soaking Sisters" — you know who you are. You all had a meaningful impact in my pursuit of writing and never failed to encourage me with the love of Christ.

To my sweet cousin, Ariela — thank you. Thank you for dreaming with me since we were kids and sharpening me through this entire journey. You're also mad talented and I so appreciate you using your skills to complete this book.

Last but not least, thank you to all of my friends who have had my back and cheered me on every step of the way. Every word of affirmation and helpful insight made this a dream come true.

Creating, writing, and self-publishing my first book wouldn't have been possible without these beautiful people's unwavering love. I feel extremely blessed to be surrounded by the best. I'm forever grateful.

NOTES

Ch 1: Identity from Intimacy

1. *Random House Unabridged Dictionary,* Brian Fiero (Dictionary.com, 1966), s.v. "Identity," https://www.dictionary.com/browse/identity.
2. Ps 139:16-18 (New Living Translation).
3. Ex 3:14 (New International Version).
4. Nm 20:12 (NIV).

Ch 2: Permission > Restriction

1. *Yes Day*, directed by Miguel Arteta (Entertainment 360, Grey Matters Production Ltd, 2021), 1:29:49. https://www.netflix.com/watch/81011712?source=35.
2. Ps 16:5-8 (NIV).
3. Ps 16:8 (NIV).

Ch 3: Tendencies, not Reality

1. Jn 15:5 (English Standard Version).
2. 1 Cor 10:23 (Christian Standard Bible).
3. 2 Cor 10:5 (NIV).
4. Mt 5:5 (NIV).
5. 2 Cor 12:9-10 (NIV).

Ch 4: Fullness > Familiar

1. Ps 37:4 (ESV).
2. Jn 10:10 (NIV).
3. Jn 14:15 (NIV).

Ch 5: Fully Affected = Fully Free

1. Prv 4:23 (NIV).
2. *Random House Unabridged Dictionary,* Brian Fiero (Dictionary.com, 1966), s.v. "Affected," https://www.dictionary.com/browse/affected.
3. *Merriam Webster Dictionary,* Noah Webster, 2nd ed. (Merriam-Webster.com, 1840), s.v. "Impacted," https://www.merriam-webster.com/dictionary/impacted.
4. Eph 3:17-19 (The Living Bible).
5. Jon 2:9 (NIV).
6. Heb 12:2 (New American Standard Bible 1995).

Ch 6: Healthy Humans

1. "African Proverb," Victoria Odoi-Atsem, accessed November 28th, 2023, https://www.google.com/books/edition/If_You_Want_to_Go_Fast_Go_Alone_If_You_W/86wxuwEACAAJ?hl=en.
2. 1 Jn 4:18 (ESV).
3. Jn 13:34-35 (NLT).
4. Jas 5:16 (ESV).
5. Prv 14:30 (ESV).
6. 2 Cor 5:16 (ESV).

Ch 7: Preference or Devotion?
1. Lk 22:39-42 (ESV).
2. Lk 22:42 (ESV).
3. Jn 15:13 (NLT).
4. 1 Jn 4:18 (ESV).
5. 1 Jn 4:18 (ESV).

Ch 8: The Dreamer & Doer
1. Jas 2:26 (NIV).

Ch 9: Relentlessly Generous
1. 2 Tm 1:7 (NLT).
2. Is 55:8-9 (ESV).
3. Community Music. "Make Room." FYWBTG Records, Watershed Music Group, 2019, Spotify song, 4:34.
4. Mt 10:8 (NIV).
5. Mt 6:22-23 (NIV).

Ch 10: Step into the New You
1. Phil 1:6 (ESV).
2. Eph 4:1-3 (ESV).
3. C.S. Lewis, Prince Caspian : The Return to Narnia, 1951.
4. Heb 12:2 (NASB 1995).

BIBLIOGRAPHY

Community Music. "Make Room." FYWBTG Records, Watershed Music Group, 2019, Spotify song, 4:34.

Lewis, C.S. *Prince Caspian: The Return to Narnia*. London: Geoffrey Bles, 1951.

Miguel, Arteta, director. *Yes Day*. Entertainment 360, Grey Matters Production Ltd, 2021. 1 hour, 29 minutes. https://www.netflix.com/watch/81011712?source=35.

Odoi-Atsem, Victoria. "If You Want to Go Fast, Go Alone." Google Books. November 28, 2023, https://www.google.com/books/edition/If_You_Want_to_Go_Fast_Go_Alone_If_You_W/86wxuwEACAAJ?hl=en.

ABOUT THE AUTHOR

Emily Ordonez is a creative non-fiction author, who pulls from her many life adventures to craft impactful and applicable take-aways. She coats hard truth with sweet tones and never misses an opportunity to share her faith. From growing up a military kid, to joining the mission field, to meeting her husband on a plane, Emily's life has had its fair share of twists and turns. Throughout every season, Emily has learned the art of growth and adaptability. She writes to empower and ignite hearts with the childlike joy for life. Though her love for writing started years ago, *Broaden Your Becoming* is Emily's first published book. You can follow her on Instagram @ordonez__emily.

www.ingramcontent.com/pod-product-compliance
Lightning Source LLC
Chambersburg PA
CBHW060532130626
46553CB00002B/721

* 9 7 9 8 9 8 9 6 0 0 9 0 8 *